Watching a Policy Maker's Back as Well as Your Own

Cory,
Thank you for your help in making this possible buddy. You are a true friend. I have enjoyed watching you grow.

—Cary McCoy

The Business of Politics Series

◆

Watching a Policy Maker's Back as Well as Your Own

◆

Carlos M. Cruz

Copyright © 2019 by Carlos M. Cruz

The Business of Politics
Watching a Policy Maker's Back as Well as Your Own

Edited by Lynn Skapyak Harlin
Layout and cover design by Richard Levine

All rights reserved. No part of this book may be reproduced or transmitted in any form or by any means, electronic or mechanical, including photocopying, recording or by any information storage and retrieval system, without written permission from the author, except for the inclusion of brief quotations in a review.

First Edition, 2020

ISBN 978-0-9740667-2-1

Cruz Concepts Publishing, LLC
5000-18 Highway 17
Suite 268
Fleming Island, FL 32003

Printed in the United States of America

To my father Carlos Manuel Cruz who never was afraid to tell me how much he loved me. He instilled a deep love of life in me which evolved into a never-ending drive to succeed while helping others along the way. His deep love of a nation which sheltered him, after losing his own, created a profound feeling of gratitude. I try to model his gratefulness every day no matter how crazy things may be. My Dad communicated his love for life every second as he created a better life for me and others. He helped me keep my feet on the ground until his death two weeks before my graduation from law school in 1995. His spirit will always guide my decisions.

Today, my wife Ryane and my children Miguel and Sebastian keep me focused on the real purpose in life.

Acknowledgments

I would like to thank God and my parents who have guided me towards wonderful accomplishments.

My wife Ryane and my boys Miguel and Sebastian make me a better person. She read every chapter in this book to me. Ryane helped me understand how to communicate with my readers while getting to know another side of me.

My friends always keep me smiling and I am grateful for them.

I am thankful for the incredible people in the Business of Politics who took the time to give me advice and show me a superior way to create changes in policy and personally achieve life-changing results.

Lauren and Jennings Depriest were my early conspirators in the development of this series. They both kept me focused and pushed me to write.

Tim Macsuga, who taught me how to understand the psychology behind my actions.

Ann Wainwright and Sharon Lybrand for saving me from myself.

Kristen Knapp and Ana Carbonell for teaching me how to interact with the media in a professional manner.

Commissioner Bob Crawford for giving me the chance of a lifetime.

Finally, my editor Lynn Skapyak Harlin hammered in the proper use of language and how to clearly express my thoughts.

Table of Contents

Acknowledgments..vii
Introduction..xv

Chapter One
The Synergistic Circle–Your Chiragon..........................1
    Why You Do What You Do Guides Your Spirit......................2
    Life Is an Interesting Journey 4
    Spiritual..7
    Family..8
    Friends..8
    Community..8
    Hobbies...8
    Business..9
    Developing Your Chiragon..9
    Your Chiragon Housing...12
    The First Step on Day One..14

Chapter Two
The Synergistic Circle–Holarchy of Need..................15
    The Absolute Trust of the Policy Maker.............................20
    Reinforce..21
    Ask..22
    Connect...23
    Correct..23
    Praise...24
    Interaction...24
    No..25
    The Complete Trust of the Policy Maker's Inner Circle..........25
    A High Degree of Knowledge of the Issues Important to the Policy Maker..27
    My Story..27

Chapter Three

The Synergistic Circle–Your Brand..................................29
    Operational Branding Protocol (OBP)....................31
    Sensational Branding Protocol (SBP)....................31
    My Brand...37

Chapter Four

Family and the Inner Circle...39
    Family...39
    Locals...43
    Friends...43
    Contributors..45
    Parties..46
    Scouts..47
    Politicians..48
    Boy Did I Anger Her..49
    Your Synergistic Circle..51
    Chiragon..51
    Holarchy of Need..51
    Brand...51

Chapter Five

Daily Dot Connecting–Stay Ahead of the Curve..........53
    Morning...54
    Me..55
    Order of Business..55
    Relate...55
    News..56
    Intelligence..58
    Nominations...58
    Guide...59
    Evening..59
    Evaluate...59
    Victories..60
    Envision...60
    News..60
    Intelligence..60
    Neutralize..61

Game Plan...61
Your Synergistic Circle...62
Chiragon..62
Holarchy of Need...62
Brand..62

Chapter Six
Lobbyists..63
Substantive...64
Hierarchical..65
Enemies..66
Locals...67
Friends...68
Balancing the Front..68
Your Synergistic Circle...69
Chiragon..69
Holarchy of Need...69
Brand..69

Chapter Seven
The Business Community...............................71
Major Donors...73
Old Money..74
New Arrivals..75
Entrenched Positioners...75
Young Up and Coming..76
Understanding Money..77
Your Synergistic Circle...78
Chiragon..78
Holarchy of Need...78
Brand..78

Chapter Eight
Parties, Leadership Players and Political Operatives....79
Parties...80
Leadership Players...81
Political Operatives..82
Time...82
Results..83

Team	83
Your Synergistic Circle	84
Chiragon	84
Holarchy of Need	84
Brand	84

Chapter Nine

Lifelong Staff	85
Subject Matter Commander	86
Mover of the Pieces	86
Creators of a Strong Bureaucracy	86
Patience	88
Questions	88
Prepare	88
Team Approach	88
Pay Attention to the Origins of Policy	89
The Long Life of Lifelong Staff	89
Your Synergistic Circle	89
Chiragon	90
Holarchy of Need	90
Brand	90

Chapter Ten

Press and the Media	91
Public Information Officers (PIO) and Communications Staff	93
Develop Key Messages	93
Develop a Communications Team	95
Press Me Not	96
Your Synergistic Circle	98
Chiragon	98
Holarchy of Need	98
Brand	98

Chapter Eleven

Takers	99
Old Friends	99
New Hires	101
The "I Want Your Job" Taker	101

The "I Know It All" Taker..101
The "I Know the Right People" Taker................102
Taken by Takers...103
Your Synergistic Circle..104
Chiragon...104
Holarchy of Need...105
Brand...105

Chapter Twelve
The Little Things that Matter Big............................107
Technology..108
Health..109
Vacations..109
Your Synergistic Circle..111
Chiragon...111
Holarchy of Need...111
Brand...112

Chapter Thirteen
Challenged Bosses..113
Loco Boss..115
Your Synergistic Circle..116
Chiragon...116
Holarchy of Need...116
Brand...116

Chapter Fourteen
Death of Your Chiragon..117
Checking Off Eradication......................................119
A Dark Place...119
Your Synergistic Circle..121
Chiragon...121
Holarchy of Need...121
Brand...121

Conclusion..123
Quick Reference Guide...127
About the Author...131

Introduction

I was in the right place, at the right time when I got my job in the Florida Senate. A State Senator took a chance on me, not because my family was connected. Fate led us to have a conversation in the emergency room of Hialeah Hospital at three in the morning. I was 19 and a junior at Florida International University, surrounded with so much love and attention from my parents. I was an invincible college student studying for the Law School Admission Test with the world to conquer.

One fateful evening I went to bed and woke up to my mother frantically calling to tell me my father was short of breath. We rushed dad to the hospital in the middle of the night. My mother rode in the emergency vehicle while I followed. The hospital was just a few blocks away from our home, yet the journey felt like an eternity.

I was in a fog and needed to find the courage to calm my mother. As I waited for some news from the ER doctors, I had an endless stream of thoughts. What the hell was wrong with my father? I felt my life would take on a new direction. I was fearful as I contemplated the worst.

"Hello Carlito, Carlito," a man called.

In that fog of fear, I heard a familiar voice. I looked up to find State Senator Roberto Casas.

"Are you, alright son?" he asked. His voice was low, his eyes concerned.

"My father was rushed to the hospital."

"What happened?" he said.

"He was short of breadth and felt dizzy."

I stared at him in my post-apocalyptic state. "I do not know what's wrong. I am just trying to figure it out. I am waiting to hear something."

I vaguely knew Senator Casas at the time. I first got to know him when he came to speak to the Future Business Leaders of America (FBLA) forum at my high school. I was president of FBLA and thought I wanted to run for office. I volunteered on a few local campaigns and began to get the attention of the political elite in the city at the time. I waved on corners for Senator Casas in his bid to fill a Senate seat left vacant due to an incumbent diagnosed with Alzheimer's disease.

"My 94-year old father is in the emergency room," he said.

He saw I was distraught.

The Senator sat down, put his hand on my back. "Why don't you come with me to see my father, and then we will visit yours."

It was such a soothing gesture I woke from my sorrow and even cracked a smile.

It felt like the walk down the hallway full of medical chatter took an eternity. We walked into a room with an energetic 94-year-old who was ready to go home. He threatened to rip the IV from his arm and call a cab. This was the Senator's dad alright; a firecracker just like him. He wanted nothing to do with his Honorable son the Senator.

"Who's this guy?" he said in Spanish.

"My father is one of your neighbors for the night, but I do not know how long the night will be," I said.

I saw his change in demeanor right away.

"Why is your Dad here?" he asked.

"He was short of breath. I have no clue," I said.

"Make sure your dad listens to the doctor and doesn't do anything crazy as he has you to live for." He pointed at me when he said this.

"Your son deserves the same," I said.

The Senator smiled. "We are going to see what the deal is with Carlos' Dad. I'll be right back," the Senator said.

His Dad laid back and stared.

When we walked into my father's room he was stable and fully cognizant. He was in good spirits, but I saw a worried look.

He smiled. "I am sorry," he said.

"Why?" I asked.

"I don't want you and your Mom to worry," he said. "This was just a simple scare I am fine." My father enjoyed meeting the Senator. After a short time, the staff asked me to go home and get some rest. I hugged and kissed my Dad on the forehead.

Later in the evening, when he was taking his Dad back home the Senator gave me his card. He passed me in the waiting room where I was still sitting trying to take make sense of the evening before getting my mom and driving home.

"Call me if you need anything." He hugged me as he left.

I looked at the card and thought about his departing words. I placed it in my pocket.

The next day my Dad was admitted to the hospital and went through a series of tests. When I arrived, I could tell he knew something was just not right.

My father flatlined when I was eight years old during bypass surgery. He had an out of body experience very similar to the myriad of eye-witness accounts you see on TV.

I did not remember the experience that took place 11 years earlier.

"Your Dad's heart is not doing well. He has to slow down," the doctor said.

"How was I ever going to tell my Father, my indestructible hero, he needed to stay home," I thought.

I was studying for my LSAT to get into law school. I was a full-time student with no full-time job. My mother was a stay-at-home mom.

"Your Dad is scheduled for surgery to implant a pacemaker. His heart is eventually going to fail," the doctor said. "To prolong his life, he needs to stop working."

My father was disabled due to the open-heart surgery he had but did side jobs to help provide for my mother and me.

"How the hell do I tell such a proud man to sit at home," I thought.

"I plan on going to law school next year," I said.

"I know, he bragged about you and told me how proud he was of you and how blessed he was to be your father," the doctor said. "You are the only one he will listen to, I hope." He smiled at me and patted my arm.

This was a not a great conversation to begin my day. I knew the real difficult conversation was still to come with my Dad.

Later that day, I hugged my Dad and found the courage to tell him the news. I knew the look on his face had nothing to do with him and everything to do with me.

My Dad lost all hope of returning to Cuba years ago and starting over. The brutal Castro regime was going to oppress the island nation for a long time. All of his hopes and dreams were in me. He had to help me get through school to live a life of opportunity and fulfill dreams he had so long ago.

"How do I make sure you do not abandon your dreams by getting a job to make ends meet?" he asked. His eyes teared up.

"It will all be fine, and I will not let you down."

I knew he felt he was letting me down. We hugged each other.

"I have options and will fill you in later after this surgery."

I only had a card with the promise from a politician who I barely knew.

"All of these guys tell everyone to call them for anything all the time," I thought as I called the Senator.

I wanted to get the rest of the storyline. I asked the Senator to have lunch as I had news about my father. I met him a day later, much to my surprise. I shared with him what the doctor said to me.

"I need a job," I said to the Senator.

He looked at me. "It just so happens that my aide is running for local office. I will need a new aide. If he wins and you are worthy, you will have a place to stay," he said. "If he loses, he will come back, but I will be able to get you situated somewhere else if you are worthy."

"What do you mean by worthy?" I asked.

"It's simple, listen, work hard, stay in school."

I was wondering where the catch was. This was just too easy.

The catch was I needed to go to school full time while I worked for him full time. I needed to stay on my law school track. He wanted to see my grades at the end of each semester. If my grades went down, I was not worthy. If my performance at work was not as impeccable as my grades, I was not worthy.

"You start now. Any questions?"

"Why me?" I asked.

I was sure the Senator had a long line of people positioning for this coveted job who were well connected and higher up on the social pyramid than me.

"I watched you when you worked on my campaign. I certainly appreciated the way you calmed my father down in the emergency room. You are hungry and have potential, now let's see what you are made of."

I attended school in the evenings and worked full-time during the day. I stayed on track and graduated from undergrad in 1990. The Senator positioned me for an incredible opportunity with the newly elected Commissioner of Agriculture in 1991, as an executive assistant. I put off law school for one year to expand my universe as an aide to a cabinet member. I started law school in 1992 and graduated in 1995. My father passed away two weeks before my graduation from law school.

Introduction

No matter how you entered the Business of Politics, you are now going to be part of a process that spans centuries. The art of surviving it in one piece becomes more difficult as our world moves faster. The Internet, text messaging, and smartphones make the art harder to master as you will be constantly pulled in a million different directions by others.

Your boss may take the form of a tax collector, city commissioner, state senator, committee staff director, congressman, or even a president. The pace, the egos, and the stakes will keep you on edge and may shake you from your focus.

I was a staffer many moons ago it seems. Back then, in 1989, portable computers were a bulky suitcase that weighed as if it was packed with clothing for a month. The Internet was non-existent, and I tracked legislation on a notepad. Online research was done while waiting in line for a copier in a legislative library. A cell phone was a brick, and no one could imagine texting.

As a young legislative aide, I looked for a guide to this staffing stuff and found nothing. There are simply no How to Books or apps that help guide you through the maze of politics and keeps you from tripping over yourself. No staffing manuscript has been written that helps you understand the obstacles thrown at you by others who prevent you from moving up.

As the years went by, several state legislative resource offices developed bulky binders with a ton of rules and useless protocols, but none addressed the full essence of the experience. If you are a staffer, this book will be invaluable. It will help you avoid the pitfalls which plague most when starting in the process. Your role as a staffer is to "Watch Your Policy Maker's Back as Well as Your Own."

My goal is to give you the mental and technical tools to navigate the business of policy making. Your interaction with people both in and out of the political process will define how effective a staffer you will become. The reputation of your Brand and the perception you create is everything. You will find this guide insightful as you need to grasp the staff psyche fully in order to advance in the world of policy making.

I am disgusted by the dysfunction in politics today. The inability to compromise coupled with the fear and drama of news outlets has created a cloud of despair in our society. All of us contribute to the lack of reason in politics because we have been conditioned to settle for less. Whether you are a politician, political staff or a volunteer on a campaign you are part of a process that was created to serve a constituency by bringing about an evolution of ideas.

How can ideas evolve when players in the Business of Politics refuse to talk to each other and just play the blame game? I decided to create the political self-help guide in order to bring clarity to this chaos and facilitate action through understanding. Politics is all around us and affects every city, village, state, province, nation or continent. You are at the center of this evolution.

I hope you enjoy this first book of *The Business of Politics Series* as it will be unlike any guide to such a crucial profession. If you are interested in a long-term career in the policy making arena or are a person in private business, if you ignore the art of politics, you will be ignored.

If you ignore politics, you will be ignored.

—Carlos M. Cruz

Chapter 1

The Synergistic Circle Your Chiragon

In the Business of Politics, you cannot afford to lose your soul. Politics is an intoxicating art form which captures its practitioners with a flow of energy that fluctuates from second to second and ensures every day will bring new challenges. There are no dull routines, no repetitive circumstances as everyday life in this profession can make or break you. Your ability to stay centered and not lose yourself is challenging, especially as you are a new student in the Business of Politics.

Synergy is defined in *Webster's Dictionary* as the interaction of elements that when combined, produce a total effect that is greater than the individual elements. Here is my definition as it applies to every individual in the Business of Politics every day of their life. Your synergy is the constant interaction of fine-tuned elements properly balanced to create an effect which enables you to succeed no matter what comes your way.

You have to be the master of your destiny. There is no way around the fact you will wake up with yourself and go to bed with yourself every day until you die. Your ability to positively communicate enables you to create an unlimited future for yourself and others.

You must learn to communicate with yourself. A synergistic circle should exist in the life of a staffer in the Business of Politics to achieve success. This synergy revolves around the following three synergistic silos:

1. Your *Chiragon* (key-raw-gone) why you do what you do which guides your spirit.
2. An inherent Holarchy of Need creating, balancing and enhancing your needs with the needs of others.
3. Your Brand credibility, perceptions, constant evolution.

Every synergistic silo is of equal importance. Each takes ongoing attention to care. You should fine tune each silo with equal passion. Think of it as working out your body, you need to balance training different muscle groups with cardio, stretching, proper sleep, and a healthy diet. If you neglect any one of these, you will not achieve your desired result or worse you'll suffer an injury.

Your Chiragon
Why You Do What You Do Guides Your Spirit

"In this synergistic silo, you gain respect for yourself."

The Chinese believe your *Chi* (key) is a life force which makes a human being alive. It's recognized by most of the ancient cultures in the world. Native Americans defined it as the *Great Spirit*. In India, it is called *Prana*. This force was central to their medicine and healing. An increase in Chi can make a sick person healthy, and those challenged enlightened. The study of Chi has evolved for over ten thousand years. It is an energy which surrounds us externally that can only be controlled by your mind. Your energy will affect others whether you like it or not so you should get better acquainted with it. How many times have you heard people referred to as having a presence which lights up a room?

Conversely, have you ever left a place because this just isn't the right feeling? Have you ever walked into a meeting with people who drain you and get you down? Do you have a friend who always seems to be consumed by negative outcomes? If you are not pumped about life, you will typically achieve little. Just ask those who suffer from depression.

Being in sync with your inner self will help you generate a positive Chi. You should feel positively charged every day to communicate the positive messages which create positive outcomes. Being excited about who you are and where you are going makes all the difference in the world. Having a positive Chi attracts great things.

In the world of martial arts, a Tiger is a young practitioner who is intrigued by the physical surroundings and external forces. Tigers are easily led and distracted. A Tiger is content one minute and growls another. A Tiger's emotions are a roller coaster of highs and lows. Tigers do not understand the path they are traveling and care less about reaching a destination. A Tiger has no sense of right or wrong as their journey is a constant maze.

A Dragon is a spiritual master of his or her surroundings and stays focused on the important things. A Dragon is defined in *Webster's Dictionary* as a mythical monster generally represented as a huge, winged reptile with a crusted head, enormous claws and teeth, often spouting fire. The fearsome Dragon, while possessing great physical strength, commands their surroundings and patiently outwits their adversary without expending much physical energy. Dragons rely on a deep spiritual understanding of the opponent. A Dragon is accomplished and has gained his wit over time. The wisdom of a Dragon makes them strong mentally, which will always outwit physical strength.

As a young staffer, you should strive to become a Dragon. The Dragon is a being who defeats his adversary without lying or cheating. The wisdom of a Dragon makes them strong mentally as well as physically. Young staffers are often taken by the movie star who shows up at the committee hearing, the reporter who is in the office waiting to interview the politician or the opposing candidate who makes an appearance at the same event. Young staffers are easily distracted and manipulated. Experience will make you strong if you listen carefully to Dragons and do what is ethically right along the way. Dragons do not engage in dishonesty.

I combined these two to create the concept of the *Chiragon:* A life force that moves your spirit. You have to find your Chiragon, the inner force which drives your spiritual being. Your Chiragon will help you keep your feet on the ground through your focused inner force.

Life Is an Interesting Journey

I had a loving childhood full of so many wonderful things. I never knew how poor my family was until I got old enough to understand our circumstances. My Dad was forced to leave his beloved Cuba due to the brutal socialist revolution and emigrate to Spain. My Mom had the opportunity to fly to Miami to be reunited with her family members who made it out earlier before the dreaded Castro storm. Whoever believes socialism and communism are the way to go is greatly mistaken. My parents had the unfortunate experience of living under the Castro regime from 1959-1965. My Dad and his ex-wife divorced due to the ruthless Castro indoctrination which outlawed religion, forbade individual rights, divided families, and confiscated property. It destroyed the individual's will to dream and achieve.

My Dad's children from his first marriage were taught to hate him as he did not embrace the new order. His oldest daughter called him a *gusano*, which means "worm" in Spanish, as he distanced himself from the growing Castro wave. Shortly after my parents married in Cuba, my Mom became pregnant and was beat up, mentally abused, and subjected to so much fear she lost the baby who would have been my older brother. My parents knew it was time to move on for their future children who would have no chance in a Castro Cuba. My mother had a son with her first husband who adored my parents. She could never have imagined the Castro regime would take this away also. Mom was assured by her ex-husband, who was a loyal disciple of Castro's army their son would make it to Miami a few days after she was forced to leave. Of course, her son in Cuba was never sent over by his father.

My father had to seek refuge in the Spanish embassy. He emigrated to Madrid, Spain. After about a year in Spain, my father made it to the states to reunite with my mom. Most Cuban exiles at the time spent several years in Spain as their paperwork made it through the bureaucracy before obtaining their exit visa.

When I was young, my father told me the story of how he impersonated a diplomat with a borrowed suitcase. He went to the American Embassy in Spain and fumbled his way through security and into the embassy. Inside, he got in line and reached an agent who was impressed he gained access as a disguised diplomat. He was also impressed by his will to be reunited with his wife in the U.S. My father pleaded with him to check his paperwork and not to have him arrested. The agent checked his paperwork and told him that all of his documents were in proper order.

"Why are you still in Spain?" he asked.

"Because it takes an average of three years to get in here to see you, but I have a wife over there that needs me."

The agent stamped his paperwork, and he was on a plane within a week. My father's inner force guided him to succeed and not get stranded in a foreign abyss.

My father reached the U.S. and got a job without speaking a drop of English. He told my mother he was here to make things work for them in Miami. A whole new struggle of life in exile was to begin for my parents, but their spirit would be free to evolve, dream, and take advantage of the opportunities the United States had to offer.

I want to earn, appreciate, and share their struggles. Their plight enabled me to have an insatiable spiritual force to succeed and to give you the tools to do the same. This is the "why" which fuels my "how to." Why I do what I do and how to do it better is a daily habit which enables me to achieve my goals. You have to find your positive spiritual force, or Chiragon. You have one already. You must identify and develop it as a beacon which guides your daily actions.

Your Chiragon also evolves. It evolves with everyday interactions which can be a happy occurrence like falling in love or a devastating life-changing accident. I have been blessed with my wife and two boys who give a deeper passionate meaning to my Chiragon. Everything I do has a flavor of my parents' plight mixed in with the force of love and laughter which engulfs my soul every second from my wife and children. Your Chiragon has a deeper, spiritual meaning than just you. If what you do only serves you, the likelihood of failure increases one-hundred-fold. There must be a higher power or purpose, a spiritual force.

The following are a few possible areas to find where the pieces of your Chiragon are hiding.

1. Spiritual
2. Family
3. Friends
4. Community
5. Hobbies
6. Business

Spiritual

I am not asking you to get on your knees and begin to pray here. What you do daily cannot just be about yourself. A higher power must exist to keep you grounded. Maybe you used to have it, and it went away. Your upbringing usually connects you to a religion or a church. Your spouse may be the catalyst for your religion now. A sense of higher power will shape the way you look at life and react to its challenges. As you get older, you will learn to appreciate it and get closer to it. Model your God or higher power. Take a few pieces of the scripture which motivate you and add it to your Chiragon. If you have no real religion, are an Atheist, or just have not made up your mind on pursuing a faith, I am sure you have a role model who influenced your life. Model them and take a few pieces of what you admire so much about them and add it to your Chiragon. What steps in this area can you take and give back to others?

Family

Family can be your parents, siblings, or lifelong friends who you call brothers and sisters. They may not share the same last name as you and may be of different ethnicity, height, weight, have green eyes where yours are brown. Typically, you have a long history with them, and for better or for worse they have influenced who you become. How can you make this relationship better? What steps can you take to be a better family member in the future? How can you give back?

Friends

Do you have a friend who is fighting a battle with Cancer, or worse, one who has a child with Cancer? How about a friend who beat drug addiction and is on a mission to help other addicts? Friends provide a wealth of add-ons to your Chiragon. If you have no friends, get some. Learn to give back to them what they gave you tenfold.

Community

Are there some charities which have captured your heart? Has your community experienced a tragic loss? Conversely, has your community accomplished an unimaginable goal? Try something which seems to be hard these days like talking with your neighbor. Look around beyond yourself, add some of these pieces to your Chiragon. Figure out how to make your community better.

Hobbies

What do you like to do? Your passion can become one of the most rewarding pieces of your Chiragon. If you are a passionate scuba diver, why not create a movement to clean reefs in your area? If you mountain bike, set up a trail for at-risk or, as I prefer to call them, at-hope kids. Add this piece to your spiritual force and give back.

Business

Have you found something you can enhance in your business world? Can you become an inspiration to others on how to balance things in and out of the office? There is much diversity in a workplace. Add this piece to your Chiragon, and maybe you can become the next great innovator in your field.

Let the above marinate in your brain as you develop your Chiragon. As you evolve (not just get older) your Chiragon can only get better. In time you will be able to see things you missed before. You will become more observant and patient. Do not be afraid of growing up.

Developing Your Chiragon

To develop any synergy, you have to start with yourself. This inner strength starts with what I call "quiet time." Quiet time is time with yourself in an isolated setting. It can entail listening to music while you write things down at home or sitting in your parked car while you enter your thoughts on a tablet. The trick is to take a good half hour at least three times a week without any interruptions. If you have an office, this setting does not usually work as there are distractions galore. Just looking at a pile of paper on your desk will get you out of your quiet state. These are the simple tools you will need:

1. Pen, paper, laptop, tablet or journal app.
2. Relaxing non-distracting setting. No phone, no texting, turn it off.

You should be able to look back at your thoughts as you evolve to stimulate more emotion and positive forward movement. Looking back can be a powerful tool for your Chiragon while living in the past is not productive at all.

I usually get stressed out when I look back at an event and decide to beat myself up for not doing something in my past. This causes me to question my present situation and fear or doubt my tomorrow. Does this happen to you? A journal, word file, note app, or even index cards can provide you with an ever-changing snapshot of where you were and help you to fine-tune your force which guides where you are going.

Your setting will be one of the hardest things to get right. I am asking you to hide from life for a whole 30 minutes per session. Back in the 1800's you could have just sat under a tree and pretty much guarantee a quiet 30 minutes. Today is quite different. Just turning off your smartphone for 30 minutes is mind-boggling, I know, but do it. All of the distractions and the noise will still be there when you turn it on again. You should find a physical place which allows you to get to a spiritual place in your mind. If you have a bunch of siblings or kids, it may be as easy as playing with time. Get up an hour early to get those 30 minutes in the dining room. You also have to make it a habit, at least three 30-minute blocks per week.

Below is a basic template of what I consider to be a quality "quiet time" session which generates your Chiragon and through repetition will help nurture and evolve it. You will be amazed at how your Chiragon will evolve.

1. Be thankful for who you are personally and professionally.
2. Be thankful for the special people in your life family, mentors, spouses, etc…
3. Be thankful for the causes, hobbies or groups you believe are in your life for a reason.
4. Picture who you want to be as you get older and wiser.
5. Picture what you can do for the special people in your life when you get there.
6. Picture what you can do with your causes, hobbies, or groups as you progress.
7. Write it all down 3-5 sentences per above numbered tasks.

Once a week, reward yourself by finding an online article, podcast, or video on something of interest. Anything comes to mind which caught your interest in the past or may get your interest in the future? Try not to make it work related. I found this to help blend in an appreciation for your newfound journey.

Sounds basic and easy? I challenge you to engage in this practice to fully understand the magic it will bring to your life and the lives you touch. I promise you the time is well spent and makes you feel more energized and alive. Your Chiragon will amaze you.

Your Chiragon is the key to keeping your feet on the ground. It gives you a constant reality check in the arena of life, full of temptations which may lead to your downfall. Your Chiragon should have a deeper meaning than just money or power. The "This is just about me" attitude will not serve you well. Being a part of the Business of Politics places you in an environment of alpha competitors who each sees themselves as the ultimate influencer. How others influence you depends on a set of spiritual core principles that evolve as you mature in life. You will also master the art of influencing others when you develop a solid Chiragon.

Your Chiragon Housing

Your mental and spiritual strength is dependent on the health of your body. The chances of advancing diminish in the Business of Politics if you are bedridden or suffer from diseases brought on by an unhealthy lifestyle. A Dragon is physically strong. Being in shape attracts positive energy from others as well as from yourself. If you wake up every morning, look in the mirror and get depressed because you "Just do not look as good as you used to," this negative energy will follow you for the rest of your day. Not looking the part you envision erodes your self-esteem. There is a direct correlation between your physical and mental health. The well-being of each must be balanced by you. The World Health Organization (WHO) defines health as a state of complete physical, mental, and social well-being and not merely the absence of disease or infirmity.

A consistent regimen of exercise is needed not only for the health of your body but for the sanity of your mind. I am going to keep this simple as you already know most of what I am going to share with you about the way you look. This advice is not going to be another one of those exercise books for the on-the-go professional. I am not going to try to sell you a miracle shake, super blender, or pill that will make you look like "Thor" or "Wonder Woman." There are four simple things you have to do to protect your Chiragon housing:

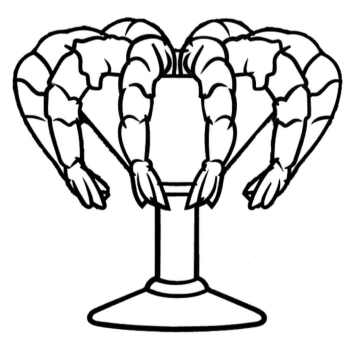

When you grow up somewhere between poor and the middle class, jumbo shrimp at an upscale event is life-changing.

1. Proper diet, eat more fruits and vegetables, lots of water, no processed foods, no junk, no fad diets.
2. Consistent work-out regimen, simple is better, no expensive gym memberships needed.
3. Rest/Sleep, I should not have to explain this one.
4. Aesthetics:
   - Dress the part.
   - Do not shake a person's hand with the hand you just used to stuff your face at a cocktail party.
   - Brush your teeth.
   - Your shoes should not have holes in them.
   - Cologne or perfume will not cover the stench of a dirty outfit or a dirty body.
   - Body piercings and tattoos should only be on display at the beach or non-formal gatherings unless you are a world-renown fashion designer or movie star.
   - Do not go too crazy with the colors of your suit or outfit.
   - Excessive drinking is not wise as slurring will slide you out of the political process.
   - Smile and make sure your teeth are not crooked.

Here is the point. As a staffer, you have to look like you belong in an arena of power. Your physique, aesthetics, dress attire, and demeanor are the first things most people notice. People tend to gravitate towards others who make them feel comfortable in a social setting. The way you look and conduct yourself should serve as a magnet that generates an interest in getting to know you. Always make a good impression.

The First Step on Day One

The first step is to leave your cozy government cubbyhole and befriend the maintenance staff. The maintenance staff will help you keep your feet on the ground at all times. A daily friendly conversational break with a person who wants absolutely nothing politically from you will help you relax and regain your center. The maintenance staff is one of the few constants in the political arena as term limits continue to sweep the nation. Political staff is constantly on the move up or out. I still see the same maintenance staff in the halls of the Florida Capitol building who used to laugh with me early on in my career. One of the most important realities most young staffers do not realize is the maintenance staff will always lend you a hand.

Chapter 2

The Synergistic Circle Holarchy of Need

If You Are Not Needed, You Will Be Gone

"In this silo, you develop an ongoing need by the policy maker for your unique abilities which are essential for your existence."

As a staffer, there should exist a Holarchy of Need which must be balanced and preserved. Without this balance, you cannot get things politically done for your policy maker on an ongoing basis. You become less valuable as staff. The concept of a Holarchy of Need is a theory in psychology created by Arthur Koestler in his 1967 book *The Ghost in the Machine*. In a Holarchy of Need, every person has value as a part of a whole which cannot exist without each individual part. The parts are crucial and create the whole, which is the sum of the parts.

A simple way to describe a Holarchy of Need is as follows. Without letters, words could not exist, sentences could not exist, and paragraphs would have no meaning. Every piece depends on the other. Here are some examples.

The love you receive from your children as well as the love you give back works together to develop a loving household. If one of your children does not love you, the entire household

Interdependence

is affected. On a baseball team, the catcher depends on the coach who depends on the equipment manager. The catcher will not do a good job if poorly coached or if he has malfunctioning equipment. Both the coach and the equipment manager depend on the catcher doing his job to have a winning season. Consecutive losing seasons will provide an exit for all three. It's a difficult concept to comprehend. This piece of the synergistic circle is difficult to understand at first. In your community, you depend on your doctor to help provide a cure as they depend on your business to keep their doors open. The pharmacy provides the medication to execute the treatment ordered by your doctor. The pharmacy depends on your doctor to issue a prescription and on you to pick up your medication. If your doctor does not give you a prescription, you will not receive your medication from the pharmacy. If you are unable to obtain your medication, you will not get better. The pharmacy will close if it does not fill prescriptions. The relationships in a Holarchy of Need slot together and have no top nor bottom as we find in Maslow's "Hierarchy of Need."

A Hierarchy of Need is a psychological theory proposed by Abraham Maslow. In his paper titled "A Theory of Human Motivation," published in 1943, he states the person or parts of the

hierarchy are based on a pyramid of simple needs at the bottom which evolves to become more important at the top.

I believe the higher you are on the pyramid, the more important and impactful your need will be. The word Honorable abbreviated Hon. is usually placed before a policy maker, member of the judiciary or a member of the executive branch. Every time I see Hon. I visualize the theory of the Holarchy of Need to stay relevant and gain upward mobility. Let's put this in the context of the Business of Politics.

In a world where the pecking order is more often than not determined by wealth, position, seniority, rank or bloodline, staff must always position themselves as an ongoing crucial part of a policy makers inner circle. Staff should be needed by the policy maker as well as the political process which creates upward mobility for them. Life in a holarchy is constantly evaluated by performance. Your performance directly affects a perceived level of loyalty.

The Holarchy of Need is the hardest silo of the synergistic circle to master. There is a high level for failure in this silo and will become a recurring problem if not properly mastered. It's this simple, "If the politician no longer needs you, the politician will move on to someone else who fulfills this need." If you fail many times with politicians in this silo, you will reach the point which makes you toxic for other policy makers to hire. It is the most frustrating experience. Here you are a staffer who has their Spiritual Chiragon in check with an established impeccable brand who watches as you get brushed aside for the "next best thing." You were there first. How can this happen? Well, it does. The cool kid in high school has to stay ahead of the new potential cool kid continuously or else he will become old news. I have experienced this personally more than my fair share and have witnessed others fail.

The Synergistic Circle–Holarchy of Need

There is always someone on the totem pole who can take your place.

The policy maker's dependence on you is everything. I cannot state this enough. The politician must balance an array of variables to enable him to get re-elected, or not. These variables are a fluid mix which range from family life to contributors, friends to enemies, and political party bosses to neighborhood grassroots captains. As a staffer, you should consistently position yourself at the epicenter, assuring these variables do not clash instead work in harmony. Some politicians are harder to deal with than others. Believe it or not they are human too.

A staffer with the proper Holarchy of Need has to have the following qualities:

1. The absolute trust of the policy maker.
2. The complete trust of the policy maker's inner circle.
3. A high degree of knowledge on the issues important to both the policy maker and his or her inner circle.

The Absolute Trust of the Policy Maker

The policy maker who hired you must have absolute trust in your ability to watch his or her back. Your goal is to become an indispensable ally with the policy maker to master your destiny. Most staffers depend on the policy maker to get elected or appointed for their very existence. The policy maker depends on your counsel to help them navigate through the myriad of challenges to ensure a

You are hired with the understanding that you have to simultaneously learn to resign.

victory at the polls. When these needs are at odds, either you will be fired, or the constituency will fire the politician.

You should bring your "A" game every day to remind the policy maker how much they need you. If you are not constantly performing in a way which reminds them of this, someone else will take your place. In the Business of Politics, the recurring theme is, "What have you done for me, and what have you done for me lately?" The Holarchy of Need is the most important concept for you to understand and manage carefully. The world of politics is constantly fluctuating, and you need to be ahead of every fluctuation, or else you will be extinct. This dependence will bring about a rollercoaster of emotions ranging from success to paranoia you have to control. While you cannot control the issues and political challenges you face daily, you can control how you respond and perform in the eyes of the policy maker. You should understand you submitted your letter of resignation before you were hired.

You have to develop a daily system of habits that continuously reinforce your worth. Follow the acronym: RACCPIN (**R**einforce, **A**sk, **C**onnect, **C**orrect, **P**raise, **I**nteraction, **N**o)

Reinforce

You should reinforce your value with key players around the policy maker carefully. The goal is to have players in the process praise you to them. Include key players as part of the solution. Reach out to them for advice and encourage open dialogue whenever necessary. Keep a running list of contact dates with the key players who are in this universe. If you do not interact with them regularly, they will feel brushed-aside. They will create chatter which does not praise you but will help tear you down. Being part of the solution to their needs in a way which triggers chatter about "how good you are" is an art. I created a list of important contacts and separated them into two categories:

Tier One This consists of the top five advisors. They may be family, contributors or consultants. You can learn over time who they are as you watch and listen. An expedient strategy is to ask. Schedule time to interact with the members on this list at least once a week.

Tier Two Everyone else. I like to keep things simple. There should be no more than 20 people on this list. Schedule time to interact with the members on this list at least once a month.

Ask

As a staffer, you cannot ask for forgiveness after the fact as it adversely affects your loyalty to the policy maker. Prior to taking action you should inform the policy maker of your future moves on their behalf, detailing all parties involved. You cannot afford to have someone else tell them what you are up to without their knowledge. This is the quickest way to lose their trust. Ask them to help you think through everything you do on their behalf no matter what their leadership style. If they tell you to "Just go ahead and get it done," detail your moves with the parties involved. You will develop a rhythm over time. You are not a mind reader and yesterday's ally can be today's uninvited guest. When I began in the Senate, I was coached by other staffers on how to get things done. I worked for a member who was not keen on details and gave me marching orders without sharing his preferred manner of getting things done. I asked while trying not to annoy. I found the best way to get an answer was by creating a list of questions and taping them to the Senator's chair. This forced a conversation. Over time, you will ask less as you gain an understanding of your political terrain. Not asking questions increases failure. Learn as much as you can about any given task and assume nothing.

Connect

Connecting dots for a policy maker to help him understand the current state of affairs is your prime objective. You must be the first to inform him of the issues and events which affect him while making connections which will capitalize on creating favorable outcomes. There can be no surprises here. If someone is going to resign, the policy maker must hear it from you first, packaged with a plan which will couple it with some gain. Your dots should grow on a daily basis. Making connections with new players and easing adverse connections with old ones will keep the trust in you growing. I made time to get together with credible players on a daily basis. This enabled me to monitor the rumors as they came to fruition. In the Business of Politics, everything begins with a rumor. Over time, I gained an understanding of the moving parts and developed an ability to predict multiple outcomes. I kept my reasoning to myself and only brainstormed with the most trusted allies prior to sharing with my policy maker.

Correct

Just as you are a sounding board for good and encouragement, you also have to be a sounding board who fine-tunes and helps correct the actions of your agency or policy maker. There can be no confrontations or disrespectful criticism. Your role is to help them become more effective at their job and point out instances where they could have done better. It must always be a positive exchange which shows them you care versus telling them what they want to hear. There will be an overload of people telling them what they want to hear as long as they are in a position of power. I respectfully critiqued the commissioner of agriculture on everything from his attire to press conferences. I would start a funny conversation prior to letting him have it. I found laughter helps policy makers better accept criticism. I would begin by talking about an awkward college football play or funny scene in a movie and then ask, "Why did you wear designer jeans and polished boots to a rodeo? You need to do much better at blending in with your constituency." Learn to politely critique no matter how passionate you are to correct.

Praise

You should be the first one to praise the policy maker for their accomplishments and encourage their ideas. You do not have to "kiss their ass" but help them to feel good about the journey they embarked on. The majority of people including media outlets, political enemies and even friends will be quick to criticize and even tear him down. You have to become a sounding board for good and encouragement. It is basic human nature to look forward to receiving praise for your actions. The policy makers I coach are no different than anyone else, praise encourages their actions and leads to upward mobility.

Interaction

You have to be in constant contact with the policy maker. Proximity is important. In an ideal world, you should be the second or third conversation they have after their spouse and family daily. Set up a routine that adapts to the policy makers schedule. Be concise and to the point catering to their needs. A day cannot go by without interacting unless you both mutually agree not to bother each other due to vacation, family events, or illness. Life will get in the way of habitual interaction. I find this to be one of the recurring failures plaguing staff. Staff will get comfortable with a policy maker and get a little lazy. A sense of security causes one to become complacent and not evolve. Consistent interaction will keep others from taking your place.

No

Saying no to a constituent or business interest is not always easy. Your policy maker, just like any other human being, generally wants to accommodate the needs of the person who is asking. Unfortunately, sometimes you just can't get it done. Instead of dragging the inevitable after exhausting all avenues, encourage your policy maker to tell them it's not going to happen. Hiding from the task or dragging it out will not gain your policy maker any favor. Encourage your policy maker to say "no" and move on. People will appreciate your trying and being honest. Remember you can't say no all of the time. If your policy maker is seen as someone who is unaccommodating to his constituency, he will be booted from his position or office. You will become an automatic casualty if you are seen as part of the problem. I try to encourage a "half no" response. "I cannot get this issue done for you but will work harder to get your other issue taken care of." You should encourage your policy maker to utilize this avenue to recover from a "no." A "half no" will keep the door open for positive interaction building longevity for you and your policy maker.

The Complete Trust
of the Policy Maker's Inner Circle

A policy maker's inner circle can make your life a living hell if not properly managed. I call this the "Drama Circle." The inner circle is the area in the Holarchy of Need which will consume most of your time. Everyone in the inner circle is well entrenched, and as far as they are concerned, you are on the outside until you prove you are worthy of being on the inside.

The problem is each of the insiders has their agenda and therefore their own subjective test you must pass to meet their standard. The inner circle requires a lot of attention, no matter how innocuous they may seem. The inner circle has the attention of the policy maker and will not hesitate to let staff know.

The easier inner circle members are those who let you know their desires from the beginning. Those who stay quiet may find ways to dispense with staff. They may dispense with staff because they were not their pick and do not trust them. As far as the inner circle is concerned, a particular staffer may have been inserted into the equation by another member of the inner circle to provide an unfair advantage.

Family, locals, contributors, parties, scouts, friends and politicians are the general categories of the inner circle. Balancing each of their needs is more of an art than you know. We will cover these in depth in Chapter 4.

For a staffer to survive, he should grow the mutual need within this circle. You should evolve as the go-to person to get anything done. You know you have accomplished the Holarchy of Need with this group when the players in the circle reach out to you constantly. The more they need, the more they will ask of you. Be mindful of your time as this group can create another full-time job in itself.

A High Degree of Knowledge of the Issues Important to the Policy Maker

Knowledge tends to be the easiest piece in establishing your Holarchy of Need. The policy maker who you work for will have an area of interest which stands out from the rest. People will call it a policy maker's passion, wheelhouse, or part of a campaign promise. The interest will guide the actions of the policy maker and all those who serve him. As a staffer, research the issue to a point where you become an authority on the matter. Analyze all possibilities and stay ahead of the research in this area. The knowledge you acquire will make the policy maker dependent on your expertise. As a staffer, you should make sure your expertise evolves and grows, which will directly affect the Holarchy of Need. The need will grow proportionately to your mastery of the issue.

My Story

When I worked at the Department of Agriculture, I was a very opinionated 19-year-old. I was cocky and came across as abrasive to some. My self-centered attitude led me to mistakenly believe the Commissioners' world rose and set with me. After a few months the proximity between the Commissioner and me was lost. Other staffers filled me in on his day pursuant to my questions and directed my tasks. Initially, my Holarchy of Need was so strong those same staffers came to me with those questions. My luster wore off due to my actions. I was fortunate another executive assistant and the chief of staff asked me to a private meeting. They told me the possibility of being jettisoned was increasing unless I changed my behavior. My face turned pale and I found myself listening for a change. Luckily, they both cared about me enough to give me a second chance. I came up with a daily process of first gathering information and then providing it as opposed to providing my advice and opinions with no basis. I developed the strategies shared in this book and learned key issues. Getting back the Holarchy of Need took a lot of time.

You will come across staff who lost their Holarchy of Need along with their job. No one in the process wants to hire them and they will eventually fade away. I look back at this experience fondly and have discussed it on many occasions with the two staffers who saved my political career. After a few months, questions again gravitated my way about the directives being implemented by the commissioner. Most of the time the simple question such as "How is the boss doing today?" reinforced my Holarchy of Need process.

Chapter 3

The Synergistic Circle–Your Brand
You Are Only as Good as Others
Perceive Your Brand to Be

"In this synergistic silo, you earn the respect of targeted players who will help you achieve your goals."

The better at branding you become, the deeper your reach, and the greater your upward mobility. Your Brand always needs to be seen as part of the solution and not as part of the problem. Branding is defined in *Webster's Dictionary* as the promoting of a product or service by identifying it with a particular brand.

In the Business of Politics, I define branding as an ever-evolving promotion of the services you can provide. Build a brand based on credibility, a smart work ethic, and create an aura about you which causes others to gravitate towards you as a crucial part of the solution.

Back in the day, you were encouraged to work hard, as it said a lot about you and your character. When your parents were growing up, their hard work would be noticed because their social circles were physically within reach and limited geographically. The Yellow Pages served as your Internet. "Your Dad was the guy who could get things done." "Everyone in town knew who the hardest working plumber was, as well as the hardest working doctor or lawyer."

Years ago, you did not need the Yellow Pages to find these hard workers as everyone in the town knew where their businesses were through word of mouth.

In today's world, your town is not geographically confined, as life has gone global. There are no Yellow Pages, and word of mouth cannot compete with social media outlets. If your brand does not evolve with the times, no one will pay attention to you. You have to post key events on Facebook, Tweet about projects, Instagram about your instant successes, Snapchat about your interaction with key players, and use whatever new mediums come online.

Let's dig deeper into a smart work ethic. Working smarter in today's world is essentially working hard, and having a branding strategy to let others know how hard you work. When I started as a staffer, there was a certain under the radar culture or humbleness associated with the Business of Politics. You could not be "flashy" nor too eager to promote yourself as it would create questions about your trustworthiness. There were unwritten rules familiar to you "listen more than you say" and "loose lips sink ships." These rules still apply today but are meant to be applied in an environment with a lot more variables. You have to work harder today to navigate through the added variables and be smarter at balancing them out.

A protocol is, according to *Webster's Dictionary*, a code prescribing strict adherence to correct etiquette. There is a particular way the society around you expects you to conduct yourself. You certainly heard the phrase "When in Rome." You have to blend, adhere, be in line, and tuned-in with your surroundings. If you, however, are just like everyone else all of the time, what will give you the edge? How will you ever get noticed?

As staff, you should brand yourself as a source for achieving a solution. You must become the "go to" person for the desired solution. Here lies the balancing act. Your brand must be subservient to your policy maker as you would not be working in your capacity but for the policy maker who hired you. Your brand is directly tied to their successes or failures just as theirs depends on your ability to provide sound solutions.

There are two types of branding protocols in the Business of Politics, Operational Branding Protocol (OBP) and Sensational Branding Protocol (SBP). Both protocols work together so if you fail in either protocol, you're done.

Operational Branding Protocol (OBP)

This protocol is under the radar, no pics, no social media, commercial free, get the job done style of Branding. The glory solely belongs to the policy maker. Under this protocol, your brand will earn a level of credibility which will be respected by your policy maker.

Sensational Branding Protocol (SBP)

This protocol is the post it, Snap Chat it, Instagram it, Tweet it, write a book about it, super bowl commercial style of branding. Under this protocol, your brand projects a level of credibility which will be respected by your targeted audience who surround the policy maker.

The best way to illustrate this is to give you a series of examples. You will be working for a policy maker in all three.

First example. You "Allen the Achiever," an aide to a State Senator and are the point person for a key piece of legislation which protects kids from bullying in our schools. The Senator made a campaign pledge to work on this issue, and it is of great importance to her constituency.

You research the issue and gain expertise on the subject matter. You also coordinate meetings with stakeholders designated by the Senator. You find common areas of agreement and have the Senator meet with effected parties, the press, and the opposition to try and craft solutions for their concerns. You work relentlessly to get a superb work product.

Along the way, the Senator commends you on your professionalism and work ethic. The people involved, who the Senator asked to work with you on this, are also impressed. Your Operational Branding Protocol (OBP) is achieved.

The stage is now set for the Sensational Branding Protocol (SBP). Everything must revolve around the Senator. You coordinate the launch of this new initiative which can take the form of a press conference, social media launch, town hall meeting, or a simple radio interview. You are the one who puts countless hours into the success of this policy change. You have to help the Senator bring this to fruition.

Continue to be part of the solution along the way as you were in your Operational Branding Protocol (OBP) by updating the Senator on constituent chatter based on interaction in the community. Come up with possible venues and a suggested list of attendees for the Senator to approve. Make sure to involve the Senator in every aspect and help her craft her speech. Use every available type of social media to capture the moment (Tweets, Snaps, YouTube videos, etc.) to let everyone know what the Senator accomplished for her community. She fulfilled a campaign promise.

Include pictures of the Senator and the interaction at the event from not only the Senator's social media accounts but from yours.

Your Sensational Branding Protocol (SBP) is achieved. Whether the Senator recognizes you or not, the targeted audience will know you orchestrated the whole thing as you were the first point of contact and focused on making the Senator shine, and not yourself.

The following examples illustrate a total failure on your part which will tarnish your brand. Once your brand is tarnished in the Business of Politics, the damage control becomes very challenging.

Second example. You are "Dysfunctional David" an aide to a local Mayor who was tasked to draft an ordinance to address a growing substance abuse epidemic. You meet with business leaders and community stakeholders designated by the Mayor to create a workgroup. You gather data, and a large portion of it comes from a new local healthcare vendor who is not close to the Mayor but is growing its footprint in the area and may afford you a position in the future. You keep the Mayor fully informed of all your progress but do not inform the Mayor of the role the new company is playing. You believe you are well positioned to facilitate a closer working relationship which will help the Mayor in the long run. You develop a superb product, and the Mayor takes notice. The people involved who the Mayor asked to work with you on this are also impressed. You work the city council on the proposed ordinance with the Mayor and get it passed.

However, one of the local physicians in the workgroup who has a competitive relationship with the healthcare vendor informs the Mayor of your inclusion of the vendor. This comes as a surprise to the Mayor. The Mayor calls you to his office and shares the conversation as well as his disappointment. Your Operational Branding Protocol (OBP) wasn't achieved, and the trust previously existed is now history.

The stage is not properly set for the Sensational Branding Protocol (SBP). You still update the Mayor on the chatter and effect you see this anticipated policy change is going to make once announced based on your interaction in the community. You come up with a venue to announce the launch of this new ordinance and a list of attendees. You work your contacts in the press and use every available social media outlet.

At the event, the Mayor does not recognize you for your work and gives all the credit to someone else. The cold shoulder does not go unnoticed. Your Sensational Branding Protocol (SBP) was hijacked as you failed to gain respect due to a lack of credibility. There is a good probability you will be moved out of the Mayor's office and fill an obscure position in some irrelevant city department. The healthcare vendor who is growing their footprint will have no interest in you now. Your credibility and access are gone.

Third example. You are "Paula Pompous" a policy aide to a congressman working with the Corps of Engineers to dredge a local waterway filled with sand due to a recent hurricane. Paula's task is to gather agency staff, business leaders, and community stakeholders designated by the Congressman. Paula presents her research to others with accuracy and passion.

She is so passionate about always being right she alienates several members of the work group. Paula informs the Congressman of the conflicts and assures him she will pass a superb work product. The frustration with Paula's, "I know everything attitude," grows within the workgroup and fuels chatter. The Congressman takes notice of Paula's challenging approach. Other staffers who may want Paula's position themselves inform him of her growing personal invincibility complex.

The people involved who the Congressman asked to work with Paula on this are counting the seconds to completion. Many hours were lost as Paula was not seen as part of the solution by the others. The work product does turn out to be one of the best-crafted plans ever submitted to the corps of engineers.

Paula's Operational Branding Protocol (OBP) wasn't achieved despite the success or failure of the proposed policy. Paula alienated people she will need in the future. They will talk to others about her pompousness.

The stage is set for the Sensational Branding Protocol (SBP). Paula immediately tells everyone how important she was in the passage of this policy objective. There is no way it could have happened without her.

Paula meticulously works on a launch strategy by covering all bases. She begins to plan a social media campaign but is assigned to a new project which entails researching behind a desk. Paula later finds out the launch took place and was a great success. Despite Paula's greatness in her mind, there was not even a mention of her name. Her arrogance obliterated her Sensational Branding Protocol (SBP). Paula's Operational Branding Protocol (OBP) is gone. Paula's actions compromised her credibility. She will now become one of those staffers who go from policy maker to policy maker over the years but will never shine.

It is so important to be part of the solution. You should understand the goal is to establish credibility for your brand with the policy maker first. Then broadcast it to a larger audience with finesse and careful attention to timing. You should keep this in focus along the way.

Everyone will test you. Territorial staff will protect their interests and all stakeholders will not hesitate to play the blame game. Be humble, smile. Always be a welcoming voice of reason. Avoid saying unproductive phrases or words such as "but," "I have been doing this for a long time," or "Why are we stuck on this again?"

It's not about you. You have to serve the policy maker first. There are a myriad of combinations we will analyze as we cover key chapters and exercises on this. The charts at the bottom of these two pages should be helpful as you visualize your path.

Below are the worst brand names you can achieve in the Business of Politics:

- I am the smartest person in the room brand.
- I am the brand name who calls you all sorts of names.
- I am the have fun not helping you brand.
- I am the more powerful than the policy maker I work for brand.
- I am only loyal to myself brand.
- I am the gossip and drama brand.
- I am the world owes me something brand.

Do you know some of these? They are in everyone's life. Your brand precedes you as you evolve. Make sure the precedent is one that empowers you.

Operational Branding Protocol (OBP)

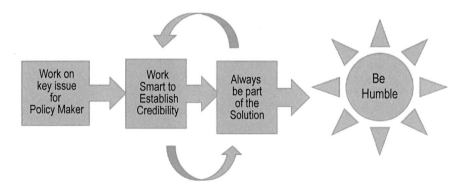

My Brand

Your brand will have some basic pillars with smaller components evolving over time. I was very young and was afforded a lot of exposure by the Senator to all of the moving pieces in his life. Every policy maker has a different style which allows you access at varying degrees. The very guarded policy maker will have you earn access to their inner workings minute by minute as opposed to a carefree policy maker like mine. I met a lot of players in the process in a short period of time, so my initial brand development evolved quickly. Here is how I believe my brand was perceived early in the process: "Very likable up and comer who is the go-to staffer for the party circuit."

I was born in Miami Beach, raised in Hialeah and was a part of the Miami fast-paced way of life. In Miami, you go out and party. When the Miami-Dade delegation staff got together during session it was usually late and long. While this was fun and allowed me to meet many people I was getting a little out of control.

Sensational Branding Protocol (SBP)

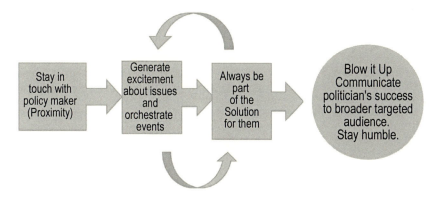

As luck has it, I was again summoned to several of those life-changing sessions. There were a few lobbyists who sat me down and gave me examples of other staffers who were known as the perennial partiers. The constant was the lack of upward mobility. The Party Brand makes you the most popular staffer who stays in their current position for decades. You do not want to have a brand which makes you popular at bars.

I hunkered down and began having more luncheons than happy hours. I met with other staffers, lobbyists and politicians who were evolving faster than the other players in the process. I always left the table with a clearly defined task I would promptly take action on. I did this consistently. My brand became so strong a position was created for me by a cabinet member. It was beyond my wildest dreams at the time. I catapulted over other staff who were in the process for years. Do not be afraid to assess your brand as you travel down this journey. Ask people who you trust both in and out of the political process to describe your brand. These "How am I doing?" sessions will make your brand take on a positive evolution. A properly developed brand will open up a myriad of opportunities.

Chapter 4

Family and the Inner Circle

The inner circle is a mix of emotional energy which gives and takes in sporadic patterns. There is no rhyme or reason for the flow of the circle. You should develop a daily discipline of habits to continuously reinforce your value to all in the circle. Family, locals, contributors, parties, scouts, friends and politicians typically comprise this circle. The inner circle will closely follow the policy maker as his or her interests will usually align with theirs. Patience and careful listening are the keys to mastering this area. Your wit, as well as your emotions, will be on a constant roller coaster when dealing with these crucial players. Breathe and get ready.

Family

Dealing with family may sound easy. In this area, your patience will be severely tested. While spouses come in a variety of personality types you will never be able to compete with them. Learn to make them your best friend. Whether they believe they are a princess, prince, the first lady of the world or husband to the most powerful person on earth because they are elected, I will show you the app for that.

The good news is most spouses tend to be just average wonderful people caught up in a world they do not understand. Your role is to help them learn to support the policy maker correctly. Start with a simple "Hello" and make certain the spouse has all of your contact info and you theirs. Set up an initial meeting with them to help them understand your role and to get to know each other. Sound simple? You will be amazed how many of your staff counterparts do not engage spouses like this. Trust me, they will engage you sooner or later if you wait, but under their terms. Touch base with them periodically and ask how you can be of service to them. Schedule time for the policy maker with their spouse as this will ensure a continual holarchy bond. Let your policy maker know every time you engage with the spouse and ask if there is anything you can improve on. A spouse is a crucial part of his or her success and will be there long after he or she is out of office. Be certain you make the spouse feel like a huge part of all the successes. It's only fair as he or she will also be a part of the failures.

The children of the policy maker will either be involved or not. Every policy maker has a different style, and you will have to adapt to it. There are typically three phases involving children in the Business of Politics:

1. The little ones, they are adorable, and everyone wants to hug them.
2. The teenager, they are either politically astute or need to be hidden away as they are teenagers.
3. The adult, predominantly helpful, loving, and politically supportive but can be the worst detriment in a politician's life.

Your role as a staffer in all three phases is to make sure the policy maker sets aside quality time with his or her family. The little ones are the best. I recommend watching where you step in the office as Lego pieces hurt if you slip your shoes off and step on one. You should have the young children at as many events as possible. Your main role is ensuring the event is young children friendly. Children help bring smiles and facilitate bonding with the policy maker's constituency. You have all seen the politician "Kiss the baby." It helps if the children like you they tend to be a good judge of character in their parent's eyes. Spend time with the children at events while maintaining your focus on the people to reach and the event's desired goals.

You do not have to be a parent to understand teenagers are challenging. Teenagers usually come in two different flavors. The berries you want to showcase or the rotten apple you want to hide. Staffers should get along with either variety.

I suppose it's human nature but staffers chose to forget they were also once teenagers. I know there is no way you ever thought you were smarter than your parents and they just never understood. You never spent more time on your hair than on the rest of your body. Keeping your car looking good was the most important thing in your life.

Make sure to position yourself as part of the solution for them also. I do not mean to let them use your place for a party. A good staffer will become a part of the family. Help guide them and teach as much as you can about the political process and life in general. Your greatest holarchy success will be in helping to make them better human beings and helping the policymaker to spend quality time with them. Schedule some time for the policy maker to take the kids to a park. Set aside a recurring time slot to play sports, enjoy hobbies with the children or attend sporting events. Encourage family vacations and outings. While you can help mentor them, there is no substitute for a parent.

Adult children are usually a very time-consuming piece of the puzzle. They are at a stage which is difficult to help mold. They will do what they do. An even-keeled successful one will blend in with the political machine and enhance it. A successful adult who credits their parents for being who they are, makes the policy maker parent complete. Policy makers who are good parents tend to be successful.

Touch base with the adult children before any event to make sure they have as much info on the event as possible. Let them know who they need to reach and what they need to say. Arm them to be successful co-hosts for their policy making parent. Let your policy maker know every time you contact their children.

The interaction with the outcast of the family will either be "Check the box brief" or "Why am I doing this for so long?" This interaction must be immediately shared with the policy maker in real time. It's human nature, since you are always part of the solution the policy maker expects you to help steer the broken ship in the right direction.

Dealing with the outcast can consume the policy maker emotionally. Always be a positive voice of reason and never judge. Judging ruins the holarchy surrounding you. Welcome the challenge and provide positive support. Consistently interacting with the adult children will enhance every synergistic silo in your circle. You never know how you can influence children. Helping to move one from the outcast silo to the successful one will not only be a great contribution to the Business of Politics but to the Business of Life.

Other family members will always be part of the mix. You will have to deal with everything from a loving mother to an estranged father. You should be needed by all as "You are part of the solution," remember. Overall, a policy maker needs to spend time with their family outside of the Business of Politics. Schedule time to visit with their aunts and uncles. They should probably regularly see their parents and attend family gatherings.

In situations where the policy maker is not married, schedule more time with their mother. Family is precious, despite what we see in sitcoms. Family helps a policy maker get away from the Business of Politics and feed their Chiragon also.

Locals

Locals are the most important group, after the family. As a staffer, you have to understand and remind the policy maker he or she took an oath to represent their constituency first and foremost. Locals expect to be seen and paid attention to or else they will vote against your policy maker. Trust me, they will let you know if you are not attentive to their needs. Some are wonderful to deal with, and some are not so wonderful. As a staffer, you should strive to develop a solid constituent outreach component in your DNA.

As the years go by, I regard helping the constituents in the Senator's district the most rewarding part of my experience. The look in their eyes, smiles on their faces replaces the look of despair due to your ability to cut through the red tape in government to benefit them. It is priceless. You will help the ablest to the most vulnerable, the children to the elderly. A piece of policy your policy maker champions which becomes a national model usually comes from an occurrence in your backyard. As a rule of thumb, "Just be nice."

Friends

Friends come in all shapes and sizes. They can be neighbors, high school buddies, sorority sisters, or business partners. Everyone wants to be a policy maker's best friend. Your job is to figure out who is truly a friend and protect the policy maker from "Friends of convenience." Friends of convenience, or FOC's as I call them, will latch on to the policy maker for what they perceive they can gain from the relationship. FOC's will try to become the gatekeeper for the policy maker and will play hardball to stay in the mix. FOC's usually have a limited shelf life as they cannot help but burn bridges.

FOC's go from policy maker to policy maker and could care less about their "so-called friend" when they no longer influence policy. You should assess their agenda and assist them when it is

Elections can be lost by one vote. Treating one constituent badly creates exponential harm.

beneficial to your policy maker or block them when they are a hindrance. Do not be afraid to tell them no or impede them on an issue. They will always come back because they know they will get something eventually. Just like real friends, FOC's tend to linger around. A straightforward to the point approach with them is usually successful. You have to create a holarchy facilitating all needs and be a continuous solution to these needs. Remember constant contact with the policy maker is key with FOC's. They will always go to the policy maker when you hesitate to give them what they want. Making sure they know why you did or did not help them before they call will grow the intensity of your holarchy with your policy maker and fortify your brand with FOC's.

Contributors

Contributors can be a mix of friends and FOC's (Friends of Convenience). They have an interest in the process whether it is for their company, community, political party, or their charity. Contributors expect to have access to the policy maker. They want to be heard and not ignored. It's simple, "If I contribute to your campaign, I expect the common courtesy of an audience." As a staffer, contributors should be handled with special care as bigger egos tend to accompany the bigger contributors. Their contributions fuel the political machine as well as your networks.

Contributors expect a return on their investment. Your role must facilitate understanding of their issues, provide access to the policy maker, and ensure the outcome is the best decision possible. Just because a contributor provided substantial funding for the campaign does not mean they get everything they want or own the policy maker. As a staffer, you will usually deliver the bad news to them on an issue the policy maker, in consultation with you, decided not to support. Properly managing the egos at every point of contact strengthens your holarchy and your brand. You should keep the door open. Campaigns will always need contributors. There will always be other issues in the future. I recommend interaction with contributors on a regular basis. You should not wait for them to make contact on an issue. Call them and let them know your policy maker is here to help if there are any issues needing attention. Alert them to issues that affect their personal or business interests. Regular interaction prevents the "he only calls me around campaign time for a contribution," stigma.

Parties

While the role of parties seems to be diminishing these days, key party operatives will always be part of the process. They help galvanize support around your policy maker and the issues they engage. Party operatives tend to bring a lot of drama to the policy making process. According to these operatives, the basic tenets of the party faithful must be the sole purpose of your policy makers existence.

As staff, you will spend time listening more to this group. Every meeting will have a standard intro reminding you of the party principles, an update on the internal party drama and a reminder of the next must attend party event. Party operatives tend to be aggressive and let their presence be known. They will usually be on a stage with the politician and expect you to treat them with a high degree of respect as they were elected by their peers.

I respect these operatives as they give a lot of their time to their party. Party operatives will usually refer constituents to your policy maker. As staff, make sure you get back to them no matter how far right or far left they may be. A staffer who can move the party apparatus in a particular direction will be very valuable to those they serve. I kept a regular tab on the party and attended important events. When a constituent with an issue came to the office and dropped a party operatives name, I always followed up with the operative to thank them and share the outcome. Invite party operatives to events and let them know how critical they are to the success of your policy maker.

Scouts

I define Scouts as agents of inclusion during a specified period. Scouts are individuals who latch on to a policy maker to accomplish a specified task. The task is usually a change in policy. They typically do not hang around the circle long. They will disappear upon the completion of their task. Scouts will migrate from policy maker to policy maker from one inner circle to another inner circle. They may be tied to an industry, a cause, or have too much time on their hands and take on a cause.

A Scout will gain entrance into the inner circle with an agenda whose deeper meaning is revealed to staff over time. They may represent a hot topic issue which will fade over time along with them. Scouts are politically astute and can overwhelm a policy maker as well as staff during this period. They can either migrate gracefully or leave a path of destruction. As a staffer, you treat them like anyone else. Position yourself as a part of the solution during the period of inner circle inclusion. Stay in close contact with your policy maker after every interaction. You may have to confront them from time to time as they will test your boundaries. I listened to Scouts and usually did not share too much as I knew their time in the circle was limited. I learned their issue and provided my policy maker with the best avenue for a solution. Scouts tend to be "name droppers" and will use your name in the future as a great example of professionalism if you help them accomplish a desired outcome.

Politicians

There will be many politicians involved in your daily interaction. The main thing is to remember that you work for one. You are the servant to an existing master and you owe your complete loyalty to the one you work for. Politicians will come in many shades and colors and typically fall into one of three categories: allies, adversaries or in-between. You must treat all of them with the utmost respect as they are elected or appointed.

Allies will be the trickiest to deal with. They will expect you to treat them with the same responsiveness you afford your policy maker. Some will claim to be the "political godfather" or "political godmother" to your policy maker. They will claim to have given birth to your policy maker's career. Some have the right to claim that, but not all. You will be able to gauge this as you interact with them. The easiest way to assess this is to ask your boss, who is who.

Avoid alienating them. They will influence your policy maker and will typically join him in their policy efforts. Your first step is to befriend their staff. Get together with them socially but be mindful you will always be an extension of your policy maker when you interact, just as they are. You are always on the clock with people in the Business of Politics. Their staff has to tell them you "Walk on water" when asked. You are always part of the solution. This will be the recurring theme for your brand.

Adversaries are easy to deal with if you know their angle. Your first step again is to befriend their staff. Their staff needs to see you as a conduit for reason when things get heated. You should cautiously interact with them. Always inform your policy maker of the interaction. You never know, you may play a role in making an adversary an ally in the future.

The in-between category should always be an opportunity to bring more allies to your policy maker's table. The members of this category are typically defined as "in between" due to being new entrants in the process. They have not had any interaction with your policy maker to determine whether they will be helpful or not. This category needs to be explored carefully to turn them into allies. Your first step is to befriend their staff. Most of these staffers will be as new as their policy maker and need help with the mechanics. You should serve as a resource for them when they are filing legislation or developing agenda items. Introduce them to support staff and show them how things get done. Always strive to be a part of the solution and help bridge differences in all three categories while maintaining a high degree of professionalism and most of all, loyalty.

Boy Did I Anger Her

My first week on the job with the Senator was eye opening. There was a special election to fill a congressional seat due to the passing of a legendary Congressman. This seat was highly contested and, in a community, as ethnically diverse as Miami-Dade the constituency was very active. I went to a precinct with the Senator to check on campaign workers. The Senator received a note from a constituent on a matter the Senator's staff was working on. I met the constituent but was in the middle of a conversation with a Councilman so I did not pay her much attention.

My lack of attention caused me to misplace the note the Senator handed me. The next day she showed up at the office and asked if I had followed up on the issue detailed in the note. I told her not yet as I had misplaced the information and she let me know how disappointed she was.

She was an older unassuming lady who rambled as she got more frustrated. I was young, third day on the job so I responded in a manner not going to position me as being part of the solution. She stormed out of the office. The next couple of days were pretty dramatic as the Senator did not like the way I handled the matter. I had no idea how politically connected this person was. She knew everyone and told everyone I was a horrible human being.

I was asked by the Senator to call her to apologize. I called but she wanted nothing to do with me. When I went to different events in the community several politicians asked why I aggravated her. People who I did not know stared at me with disgust. Even the Mayor's wife and daughter asked me how I could have done such a thing.

I found out later this person who I angered was a friend to many, key political operative and a local under the radar political machine. Not bad for week one. I worked extra hard on getting the best outcome for her as possible. I dove into her constituent issue and solved it. I called her and she was very pleased. The following week I said hello to her at an event and she praised my efforts but said she still did not like me. I worked until I won her over, but it took a long time.

Your Synergistic Circle

You have to navigate and manage a policy maker's inner circle successfully.

Chiragon

You have to understand your inner circle to deal with someone else's. Follow your values and be guided by your spirit.

Holarchy of Need

All of the players in the circle must see you as a needed piece of the circle which is fluidly favoring no one particular piece more than another.

Brand

As the players in this circle acknowledge you as being part of the solution, it will be reinforced by circle members and come back full circle.

Chapter 5

Daily Dot Connecting
Stay Ahead of the Curve

Life as a staffer is full of excitement. Every day is always different. It's a roller coaster ride, you are at a peak one second and come crashing down in the next. Politics and policy making is a dynamic process. A certain set of skills sharpened routinely, will make you more efficient. This practice will serve as a primary tool to help you move up in the Business of Politics.

Being able to make connections to influence outcomes is the practice of Connecting the Dots. You have done this in the past, but it was not clearly defined as a business tool. For example, before asking a person to be your date at your high school prom, you asked her friends to say good things about you. You may have influenced some to help get to know her brother or sister. Did you ask some friends to help you get to know her parents? By gathering relevant information about her and having people she cared about say good things about you helped create a desired outcome when you got the nerve to ask. I hope she said yes. I will use high school examples from time to time in order to illustrate concepts in the Business of Politics. The more you practice this, the easier you will be able to maneuver and connect the dots. You have to wake up every day and go to bed every day, connecting dots and assessing their impacts or consequences. After a while, you will develop an ability to predict things as well as to foresee available options. You cannot afford to have your policy maker blindsided or be the last to know.

The death of a key supporter, the resignation of a political enemy, the announcement of a scandal, or an environmental disaster must filter through you well before everyone else knows. If the daughter of a prominent businesswoman in your back yard gets into Annapolis, you should be the first to inform your policy maker to reinforce your holarchy and brand. You are on the front line. The ability of the policy maker to stay ahead of the curve must be dependent on you. These habits will help you in the private sector also. The successful executives master habits which catapult them to the top. *Webster's Dictionary* defines habits as a behavior pattern acquired by frequent repetition or physiologic exposure that shows itself in regularity or increased facility of performance.

You know me and acronyms. The acronym for morning is MORNING. Try to guess the acronym for evening. You got it, EVENING. Below is the breakdown.

Let's break this down into morning and evening dot connecting sessions.

Morning

M e
O rder of business
R elate
N ews
I ntelligence
N ominations
G uide

Me

When you wake up, take care of you. Start with your quiet time and focus on your Chiragon. Ask yourself the questions which keep you centered. Your focus on what makes you the person who you are and how you plan on evolving to the next level, must be first. Work out and take care of your body as well as your mind. Align the Holarchy of Need as well as your brand.

Order of Business

You should have a schedule with a task list that needs to be completed by you to help your policy maker (e.g. department head, county manager, or mayor) achieve the goals of the day. Try to be thorough while keeping things simple. If using an electronic medium to manage the tasks, use a personal account to avoid making public your strategies and techniques. Developing a thesis is not the goal here. This list is simple and ever evolving. Daily life will get in the way of checking things off. Be mindful of letting the important things interrupt your flow as the tasks will still be there the following day. Plan for contingencies and breathe.

Relate

Every action taken should relate to a subsequent one designed to connect dots for your policy maker. You are the enabler whose events must yield relative gains. A simple meeting over coffee should have a follow-up action which connects another necessary dot. If you are working against a policy initiative on behalf of your policy maker, meetings and phone calls should relate to the purpose of defeating the legislative matter. As constituent groups sign on to help your policy maker ask them to help you connect with other groups which can be helpful. If your policy maker is seen meeting with a political ally it will make political enemies uneasy. Conversely meeting with a political enemy will create angst in political allies. Staff will orchestrate the timing for these actions in order to create a desired result. Understand the possible outcomes of every step. I try to consider all preferred outcomes of a particular action first and then analyze the negative possibilities. Over the years, I have developed a system of running scenarios by a handful of trusted friends. I am always surprised at the additional insight brought forth by this exercise.

News

Headlines change every second. You have to establish a system which informs you of events in real time. There are a myriad of apps for this. The real magic lies in hearing about things before it becomes news. Having credible friends in the media inform you about a story before it goes live will pay dividends with your policy maker. Today's media runs on fear. Everything seems to be negative. Policy makers fear having a bad article sneak up on them. Time to prepare and counter a negative article is priceless. Get both sides of the story as every media outlet has their "fear" spin nowadays. The talk show hosts need to create some drama to sell their books. If you listen to a conservative or right-wing outlet, make sure you spend equal time getting the view from a liberal or left-wing outlet. Getting the full picture creates a balance to understand the issues from multiple angles.

The downside of constantly analyzing the media in the Business of Politics is you will no longer relax while sitting down and watching a news program. It will become part of your job. Blogs, podcasts and you tube channels are also helpful.

Understanding the angles will arm you with a more global understanding of current events. It will enable you to maneuver and gain favor with your policy maker. I find myself being one of those

Daily Dot Connecting–Stay Ahead of the Curve 57

patrons in the supermarket who looks at all of the gossip magazines while waiting in line. I laugh. This is the only news I have no desire to analyze.

I have a supermarket line subscription.

Intelligence

While you progress, you will establish a network of sources which will share information with you. Sources can be institutional staffers, credible reporters, powerbrokers, and the business community. You should be in constant contact with your sources and feed them with helpful information as they will, in turn, feed you. Whether you get intel on a specific policy area or an unforeseen shift in political leadership, you should not be the last person to know. Getting the scoop first enables you to position your policy maker to make the shift. He will have more time than others to adapt. Everyone has friends who hear things before others. Reach out to them on a regular basis. Make it a point to not always call for information. Call to wish them a happy birthday also.

Nominations

Facilitating coveted appointments to a board, task force, department, or agency can yield years of compounded influence. Nominating others for key appointments is an underutilized tool. Understanding and working with the appointee process to key boards or positions must not be overlooked. You not only need to know who else is in line, but you need to help key supporters get these coveted appointments. The more allies you can help place in key positions, the greater your influence, and job security. Keep an updated list of potential nominees whose interest can be activated and paired up with an opening. Constantly recruit talent in crucial areas of concern to your policy maker. You can also have your policy maker create a task force or special committee to address growing concerns.

Guide

Your guidance every step of the day to meet any challenge or to capitalize on opportunities is not only expected, but it's why you are employed. This morning set of habits must be consistent. Your sole purpose in doing this is to add tools to your universe which can be used at key stages to benefit your policy maker. Your morning routine will create incredible value. It will enable you to guide your policy maker in the right direction.

Before going to bed, you should reflect on the day's actions and prepare for the actions of tomorrow. Giving thought to your actions and the outcomes will further sharpen your staffer abilities. The challenges dealt with on any given day will lead to subsequent relative solutions if properly analyzed. Do not take failures or wins personally. As staff, you are a cog in a multi-faceted machine. Whether positive or negative these outcomes exist to realize subsequent ones. I use the acronym EVENING for the evening routine.

Evening

E valuate
V ictories
E nvision
N ews
I ntelligence
N eutralize
G ame plan

Evaluate

The morning begins with you. So must the evening end with you. Trace your day as a staffer and ask yourself, "What could I have done better? Did you lose it with anyone? What gains did you make in your Holarchy of Need? Did your Brand suffer?" Do not dwell on things or beat yourself up. Learn from them, and all tomorrows will be better.

Victories

Go to bed, focusing on your victories. They will help you sleep better. There are victories every day. Unlike our negative press outlets filled with fear, you can find and report your victories with your special spin. Go to bed ready to build on the platform you detailed today to better serve tomorrow.

Envision

Envision your tomorrow as a productive continuation of your today. No matter how bad your today was, there will always be a new tomorrow. Picture your tomorrow as a perfect day. "What would make tomorrow a better day? What variables do you have to help align?" Live it in your mind. Visualize tomorrow as an opportunity to shine for yourself as well as for your policy maker.

News

Try to get ahead of tomorrow's news with the information gathered today. Anticipate possible outcomes by reviewing what you have. You must understand how to direct your policy maker to benefit from the headlines by mentally compiling your intel in order to provide additional perspectives when you wake.

Intelligence

Ask yourself what useful intelligence was gained by you today and from what source. Sources get better and sometimes get worse on any given day. Are you treating your sources with the right amount of attention and care? Sources who are consistently unreliable should give way to new reliable ones. Reliable sources need to be periodically recognized and praised. Take them to dinner or out for drinks. Be sure to pick up the tab.

Neutralize

Will you be prepared to neutralize harmful situations? What armed you today to better deal with tomorrow? Who will you choose to stop unnecessary drama? What can you use to your advantage to turn weaknesses into strengths? You have to feel confident in your abilities, or you will fail before you even wake up.

Game Plan

Look over your schedule and task list for tomorrow. Make a quick mental note of it and go to bed. Tell yourself "I am outrageously prepared but cannot take care of it until tomorrow," or else you will find yourself up all night.

The first rule for the above habits is they must be consistent, or they will not become habits. The second rule is to also take time off for you. I know this sounds impossible but try to turn things off and focus on what matters to you and not the policy maker from time to time. You will need to recharge your soul by enjoying friends and family who do not care about politics and who you know.

There will be weekends where you have to work as crucial things develop. There will be periods such as a legislative session where you will sacrifice countless weekend hours. Every weekend cannot be crucial. If you do not take time to disconnect, you will burn out in a bad way. The Business of Politics is unforgiving. A negative outburst due to being overworked or fatigued can create a quick exit from politics for life. How many staffers have you seen resign ever truly bounced back? They are few and far between. You will hear they are now selling real estate or end up working for their parent's business. They are damaged in the profession.

Your Synergistic Circle

You must consistently identify and capitalize on opportunities for your policymaker by engaging in a series of daily habits.

Chiragon

You should to be guided by your values as you face the day-to-day process of policymaking. Stay calm at all times to project solution-based leadership.

Holarchy of Need

Your circles must provide you with timely information. This will give you a window to evaluate and properly guide your policy maker to take the correct course of action.

Brand

You cannot afford to have events blindside your policy maker. Your Brand will get stronger with opportunity as your ability to watch their back increases.

Chapter 6

Lobbyists

I know I may sound biased, but credible lobbyists are an excellent source of information and can help facilitate good policy outcomes. Lobbyists are demonized by the press who forget to tell the public they also hire lobbyists, believe it or not, the press is a special interest. In the Business of Politics, lobbyists tend to be a small clique in any given area. Most lobbyists will know or have heard of each other. Most of your state lobbyists know the other state lobbyists. Even at the Federal level where there are many more players from all over the country, there are small cliques in respective industries, the agriculture, energy, the Close to the President and the Old Player's clique. The lobbyists in play will change with administrations. Who's in charge and a lobbyist's proximity with the policy maker will usually determine how many clients they have in the private sector. Lobbyists can work for smaller boutique firms, mega-conglomerates, iconic law firms, not-for-profits or foreign governments. Some can be parents who have suffered an unimaginable loss and have taken on a cause to make the world a better place.

You must understand the different lobbyist types to further the agenda of your policy maker. Managing the traffic in this area was one of my most challenging roles as a staffer. Most of the lobbyists in the corps were lobbying since before I was born, and many will let you know that on occasion. Lobbyists are an excellent resource for staff. Lobbyists will typically fall into five groups that will be important to your policy maker. The acronym for this is **SHELF**: **S**ubstantive, **H**ierarchical, **E**nemies, **L**ocals and **F**riends.

Substantive

Substantive lobbyists are the subject matter experts. They are seasoned veterans of the lobbying corps and can work in either the private or public sector. Most have written or helped write most of the law in their respective areas. They have a high level of credibility. Their reputation is impeccable.

Substantive lobbyists have mastered the key intricacies of their subject matter area. A Substantive lobbyist wants to know, in their mind, they are an indispensable resource for the policy maker. Most Substantive lobbyists are old school. They tend to be loyal and stay friends with you a long time after you win them over. Staffers must create a solid relationship with Substantive lobbyists in the areas assigned to you or in the areas most important to your policy maker. Use the Substantive's knowledge to design and craft innovative solutions. This will further your policy makers agenda as well as your own.

I became good friends with the lobbyists who worked in industries important to the Senator and his constituency. I found it helpful to understand healthcare to address the needs of our constituency. The lobbyists in this area not only shared their knowledge of the issues but were able to help solve constituent care issues with the providers they represented.

Hierarchical

The Hierarchical lobbyist will have the largest ego of all the groups combined. In their mind, there is a direct correlation between upward mobility and them. They think they are the reason why your agency head or policy maker is there in the first place. Others usually credit them for getting your agency head appointed, or policy maker elected.

Make sure you learn to distinguish who a real power broker is. There are many lobbyists who project a false sense of importance. Hierarchical lobbyists tend to trend up or down depending on how close they are to the current leadership. A Hierarchical lobbyist will have an innate ability to out maneuver others to further their desired agenda. Their ability to adapt is impressive. They will morph into a new political camp faster than you can imagine. The Hierarchical lobbyist comes in three different types: Flashy, Shady or Classy.

The Flashy Hierarchical lobbyist is loud, eccentric, overpowering, and loves to read about themselves. The Flashy type is social media-centric and lets you know how important they are to your universe. Do not let their eccentric nature fool you as the Flashy lobbyist has a bite. They are effective and have consistent policy wins. The Flashy covers his bases by directly interacting with the politicians. They will typically hold court in their office or an old establishment restaurant. Admission is by invitation only.

The Shady type had their best years back-in-the-day. This type made money and were at the top of their game but got too comfortable and stopped evolving. Some may have gotten too greedy as they rose to the top on the coat tails of a prior policy maker. They long to relive those days and are always looking out for the new up and comer. The Shady client list is typically comprised of a handful of old clients who keep them as a matter of loyalty.

The Classy type tends to function under the radar and hates to be in the press or on social media but likes everyone to know they make things happen. The Classy will listen more and will keep a consistent demeanor throughout your interaction. They are warm, inviting, and are known for their disarming charm. The Classy is usually several steps ahead of the others when planning policy changes. Strong ties to lifelong staff comprise a lot of their power. They cover their bases with staff and politicians.

Both the Flashy and the Classy will be consistently effective and will usually stay close to your policy maker if they see long term potential. The Shady will either be really in or really out. The Shady does not last as they cannot help alienating policy makers and staff. Keep in mind, the consequence of not managing the Hierarchical lobbyist may indeed be downward mobility as they are constantly advising your agency head or policy maker and will have an influence on key decisions.

Enemies

Enemy lobbyists can come in the following three categories:

1. Those who hate your policy maker but must play nice in a public arena.
2. Those who have a horrible reputation for lying.
3. Those whose represented interests do not align with a policy maker's agenda or values.

You need to be seen as a consistent part of the solution. The lobbyists who hate the policy maker or agency head you work for can be charming but will use any means to bring your policy maker or agency head down. You can be courteous but understand there is no fixing the interaction, as things tend to be too ideological or personal.

Lobbyists with a horrible reputation earned it for the most part. Their credibility level will usually remain at an all-time low until you hear of an interaction bringing them even lower. Try to avoid wasting too much time being a saint with these first two categories of enemy lobbyists. You will only help them set you up for failure.

The final Enemy lobbyist category is fluid, depending on the times. This category can be aligned with your policy maker or agency as current events unfold. Don't take it personally, lobbyists who work on issues you do not agree with have to make a living too and they have a family to feed as well.

A good example can be when groups which tend to be mortal enemies come together to fight legislation against a common foe. It does not happen often, but it does happen. You must always keep an open line of communication with groups on the other side in a respectable manner. Your policy maker or agency head will eventually need to work with the lobbyists for these groups. You always have to facilitate a solution. You will have to identify who the best lobbyists are in the mix as there will be radical voices within this enemy category. You should get to know the reasonable ones and keep an open line of dialogue with them. Do not try to work with the extremists as they are always right in their mind and have no intention of working towards a solution.

Locals

Lobbyists who represent local interests will have a natural affinity with your policy maker. Your local cities, chambers, law enforcement, veterans' groups, and key charities are part of the constituency. They are local and must have a front row seat at all times. Locals tend to socialize more. You must manage the time involved with local lobbyists. Local lobbyists tend to hang around in your office more and while pleasant, can waste a lot of your time. As a rule of thumb, the office is for conducting business, and socializing should be done at a restaurant or the local watering hole. I worked on many local issues with lobbyists from the Senator's district. I learned to manage them by tasking them with things which helped me help them. I kept a list and held them accountable. Keeping them busy trying to help themselves gave me time to help others.

Friends

If a lobbyist is a true friend of the policy maker or key ally for an agency, they should always be welcome. They have known your policy maker a lot longer than you. A friendly lobbyist can be Substantive, Hierarchical, or Local. Beware of your ego with this type. Staff who tries to adopt a protectionist philosophy against friends may be unemployed. Be careful not to try to discredit a friend unless you have solid proof and other friends will step up and back you. The worst thing you can do is make enemies, which takes away from your ability to be part of the solution at all times.

Balancing the Front

Despite the crazy news outlets which run on fear, lobbyists are an invaluable part of the policy making process but being on the front line with lobbyists can be very intimidating.

The first committee week in Tallahassee I traveled up with the Senator. I was the only person staffing his office that week. I had to direct and control the flow of access. Most of the visitors introduced themselves and were extremely pleasant. There was one lobbyist who walked in, ignored me and barged into the Senators office. I got up and went to pull him out of there and the Senator introduced him to me. The lobbyist was a local from Miami-Dade. He apologized. He thought the staff was back in the district. He did not know me. I thought the lobbyist was a little pompous but just shook his hand. Despite this rocky first impression, I always tried to be a part of the solution on issues represented by his firm. He was well connected and extremely well versed on the issues he advocated for. I used him as a source of valuable information as I researched and analyzed issues. Over the years our friendship grew, and he remains a valuable source of information today.

Your Synergistic Circle

You have to successfully navigate and manage lobbyists in your arena.

Chiragon

You cannot be partial to the interests they represent and must keep an open door with those who respectfully disagree.

Holarchy of Need

All of the lobbyists must see you as the front-line conduit who regulates their access.

Brand

You must come across as very credible and close to your policy maker. Lobbyists need to trust that sharing information with you is just as good as sharing it with the policy maker. This will ensure a level of high respect.

Chapter 7

The Business Community

Every region has a handful of key industries that are the financial heart and economic soul of the constituency your policy maker or agency serves. This community tends to run in a close-knit group and act in concert. The business community has pillars within it who will be the face for interaction and political asks. These faces never seem to change but will evolve with new additions and very few exits.

I know very few policy makers or agency heads who have alienated their business community and survived. Your interaction with the business community must be handled with the utmost care.

I use the acronym MONEY to help define the categories of business community players who you will encounter. There are five main categories of financial players in the Business of Politics:

M ajor Donors
O ld Money
N ew Money
E ntrenched Positioners
Y oung Up and Coming

Money

The Business Community will have its universe of drama as positioning for the next chair of the top local charity or securing an appointment to a coveted board will pit this elite class against each other. The drama tends to fizzle after it is all said and done until the next positioning exercise.

You will encounter personalities who range from Old Money to the new millionaires who just sold the App they created in a garage. There usually is a traditional way of doing things tied to a region as Money predecessors set a precedent or rules of engagement.

In some cities Money tends to wear ties and deals are brokered over an expensive dinner. While in a trendy metropolis like Miami no one wears a tie and deals are brokered over a Mojito and a cigar. When in Rome act as the Roman conquerors or else you will be conquered.

The Business Community has a key group dynamic you have to understand as a staffer. Different tribes do not always see eye to eye but come together in times of challenges and crisis facing the community. You have to understand the personalities in each of the following categories and bring them to your side.

Major Donors

The players in this category put their money where their mouth is in a big way. This category is the smallest. There are usually the same 5-10 players in every community who can raise a lot of money for everything from charitable organizations to funding a Good Samaritan heart transplant. Their power comes from the policy makers who rely on them not only to fund their campaigns but to connect them with key contacts to facilitate positive political mobility. This category also directly impacts those appointed to key agency positions as the origin of appointments are usually tied to players in this category. There is usually very little doubt as to who is close to who in this category as Major Donors are usually close to everyone and anyone they chose.

The more allies in this category, the greater your rate of success will be with the business community. Spending time with this category will develop a surge of interest from the other business community categories. Mastery of this category alone will enable you to effectively align your agency or policy maker with the business community and help you successfully achieve your goals. You should always be seen as a conduit to positive outcomes and solutions by the entire business community in order to achieve a balance and not alienate the others. The Major Donor category can be captivating for young staffers. They are directly responsible for political victories as well as defeats. Many young staffers mistakenly believe these donors will pave the way for movement up to the next level. Moving up in the process is a balancing act which requires attention to all the money categories. Do not solely focus your efforts in this silo as tempting as it may be.

Old Money

The players in this category may or may not put their money in helping your policy maker with their campaign. This category features a cast of players whose names adorn street signs and old institutions. Key university conference centers, local parks, and even pee wee baseball teams bear their designations. You can only be born or married into this category. This status is always achieved from within the current players. Some chose to be involved in the Business of Politics directly or indirectly through surrogates hired to represent their family fortunes. Their ties to one another are deep as they all grew up together and attended the same schools. They are usually bound to each other through established family ties. The children of this category court one another, and many power weddings are the fruit of this interaction.

Identify the players in this category who are actively involved in making things happen in the business community, whether it is for the betterment of the business community or themselves. Active Old Money players can be a catalyst for positive growth. They can cross over into the major donor category from time to time to help your efforts not just when one of their family members is seeking political office. Do not waste time on Old Money players who wake up and breathe with an abnormal opinion of themselves. They will not help you as they are only interested in funding the past, their old alma maters or key charities which bear their names.

New Arrivals

The players in this category usually emerge from corporate relocations or expansions into your region. Large corporations are courted by communities to bring jobs to their areas which facilitate an overall positive economic impact. They usually bring a handful of key players who will add to the business community elite. They may choose to become a Major Donor in selected endeavors as their corporate culture permits.

A New Arrival buzz will lead to a frenzy from the other business community categories. Even some in the Old Money category will want to meet the new player in town. Money is usually budgeted to make a big splash right away as a new arrival has to show the region they mean business. A New Arrival may not be infinite. Their presence may be redirected by a corporate merger or a better offer by another region which would like to be graced by their presence.

You should place your agency or policy maker in line to meet them as soon as possible. You have to act fast. Have them believe in your policy maker's ideas and vision before others position themselves higher in the pecking order. The New Arrival will become old news and will gravitate into one of the other business community categories except for the old money. The process will start all over as the business community makes way for the next new arrival.

Entrenched Positioners

Some in the business community have a keen ability to position themselves as a player on a given issue at a given time. They want to be part of striking a deal. I call these Entrenched Positioners. They always manage to be part of the mix. Entrenched Positioners will never become Major Donors but will ally with Major Donors from time to time to get them to the table. The long-term players in this business community category are credible and crafty. Entrenched Positioners are the most aggressive of the business community categories. They do not have the resources of the other categories and rely on being a few steps ahead to slide into position.

This category can be used to forecast movement in the business community. Entrenched Positioners will usually know of the next New Arrival or drama in the business community before anyone else. You have to be able to get up to the minute updates from a handful of Entrenched Positioners to create a system of checks and balances. Your agency head or policy maker will greatly benefit from forecasting movement in the business community. Beware of the one-shot Entrenched Positioners who benefited from past deals leaving behind a trail of carnage. They will try to turn the tables on you to help position themselves with your Brand as this may be the only thing they have left. Avoid the one-shot Entrenched Positioners.

Young Up and Coming

The New Kid in Town always seems to have attention gravitate towards them. Young Up and Coming business community members are usually hard workers who charm the other categories of the business community. Other category members see a lot of themselves in them. The "you remind me of myself many years ago when I started" aura is a magnet for business community members to help groom and cultivate. Members of this category tend to be younger and full of charisma. Young Up and Coming members usually make a splash with a start-up enterprise or position themselves with other business category members, mainly Major Donors who open doors for them.

Befriend Young Up and Coming who align with Major Donors and help to mentor them just as the Major Donors are. Help guide them to align with your agency head or policy maker with a feel good endeavor which will benefit the business community. You must create a strong bond with someone who may ultimately become your boss as these Young Up and Comers do grow up.

Understanding Money

The business community is an integral part of a region's success or failure. We are blessed to live in a capitalist society where we look to the private sector for solutions as opposed to growing government into a socialist state. I lived in two key regions in Florida and saw good policy solutions developed when the business community came together.

You should get to know the key business players in your area. Make a list. Get together for lunch or other social gatherings with business leaders. Find out what drives them. Most of the players in the business community will share knowledge and strategies. Do not hesitate to ask questions. They learned from others who took the time to teach them. Learn from their successes as well as failures. Let your policy maker know who you meet with and give him your honest assessment of the individual. Keep your interaction discreet. This community is tightly knit.

I am not enamored by money. The most successful business minds tend to be the most down to earth. I always focus on getting to know the person and not their wallet. The overwhelming majority of people in the money community are good people and you should gravitate towards them as they will gravitate towards you if you are a good staffer with a good Chiragon. A bad person will be bad regardless of whether they have money or not. Stay away from the bad money players just as you should stay away from any bad influences in life. The bad money players have the resources to ruin you faster than you think. They will influence others using their money and network resources to create a rising tide against you.

Your Synergistic Circle

You have to effectively learn to bring the business community over to your policy maker or align them with the efforts of your agency.

Chiragon

It's not about how much money but about the quality of the business community member's interest in helping your policy agenda.

Holarchy of Need

All of the players in the circle need to see you as a close ally who favors the players in no one particular category more than the other.

Brand

The constant message you need to have circulated is each of the players in their respective category thinks the world of you.

Chapter 8

Parties, Leadership Players and Political Operatives

Policymaking is ever evolving, and partisanship will play a role in some things. It cannot be the overbearing influence in all things. This will lead to stalemate and dysfunction in the political process. Sound familiar? How functional is a congress that provides no real solutions due to political gridlock? Congress is unable to come together and pass meaningful legislation. Not even a bipartisan budget.

Party worship and loyalty evolved in your family over time as today's family Democrat may have been yesterday's Republican. Your parents may have been Democrats because their parents loved John F. Kennedy. Your great grandfather may have been a Lincoln Republican but some of your great uncles where proud supporters of Franklin Delano Roosevelt and his democratic New Deal.

Today's party system evolves faster with social media and our ever-evolving technology. The passions, personalities, and leadership players must be understood to help your policy objectives.

The greatest policy makers of our time worked with members across the aisle to create positive outcomes. President Reagan, a

Republican, successfully worked with Speaker Tip O'Neil, a strong Democrat. President Bill Clinton, a Democrat, worked with speaker Newt Gingrich to accomplish monumental reform. You are a conduit to bring about positive solutions for your agency or policy maker. Do not sell yourself short by navigating with party blinders which will prevent you from achieving good policy outcomes for your policy maker.

Parties

As you mature in the process, you will realize political parties do not always define a policy maker. Taking a purely partisan approach to politics is short-sighted. You must align yourself with your boss's ideals, not a party label. You have to be a professional first and keep the lines of communication open with all parties in the process. Once you are in the Business of Politics, understand the policy solutions you help formulate, such as litigation reform or the passage of new environmental regulations, are typically not embedded in some best-selling book. There is no political convention template. Good policy formulation happens when all reasonable parties participate in a solution.

Current events will galvanize issues around a party platform as opposed to a party platform galvanizing current events. A school shooting will bring about a national debate dictated by opposites in respective parties. The policy solution you will help formulate has to be a pathway to common sense. Parties will have voter strongholds in different regions. The greater the number of registered voters for the respective party, the greater the influence the political hierarchy will reflect. Your agency head or elected official will deal with the party drama. If you directly engage in the party rhetoric, your life as a staffer will be short-lived. There is no place for constant party activism when you are advising your agency or policy maker to bring about solutions. Be mindful of the party mechanism and how it will affect the implementation of the policy solution which you help develop. Use your party contacts to gain intelligence and not to plan the next rally. It's simple. If you want to be more of a Republican or Democrat than someone else, run for office.

Leadership Players

While leadership is priceless, the political leadership in any given arena will make you pay the price if you are not aligned with their vision of policy. The consequences may mean a demotion for your agency head or the loss of a key chairmanship for your policy maker. You must provide the mechanics that will script the evolution of your policy maker's leadership ability. Your goal is to facilitate upward mobility for your agency head or policy maker. Leadership players such as a Speaker of the House, Senate President or County Manager will usually dictate the direction of policy in their respective realms. When you upset them it is usually a combination of not truly listening or understanding their expectations while taking a policy stance without properly communicating. The adverse consequences tend to be immediate as your agency head or policy maker will have a sudden fall from grace.

Getting back in good favor with leadership players will usually take a long time. You should understand the values and direction of your leadership hierarchy. Staff must advise on the political consequences orbiting a proposed solution. You must preach patience and methodical steps to be taken before having your agency head or policy maker schedule a press conference on a new policy announcement. Develop a system of checking off the boxes with key leadership players to get their approval and their blessing.

Political Operatives

A campaign has paid campaign operatives such as pollsters, media consultants and campaign managers. Campaigns also have a myriad of volunteers. Campaign staffers usually get rewarded with coveted political positions in government agencies after a successful campaign. These range from the scheduler to Chief of Staff. The problem is most campaign staff are good at running campaigns but horrible at running government organizations. You will work with or for one of these appointees at some point. Being a government employee can be challenging for campaign staff. The ones appointed to these coveted positions typically fall into two extremes. The one who gets how government works and the one who does not.

There are simple explanations for either extreme as the day to day techniques used for campaign management versus the management of a city, county, state or federal entity are opposites. Analyzing the key differences will enable you to better interact with them. They will impact your upward mobility no matter how long you have been in government. The following three key variables will lend some insight into understanding how to navigate with a Political Operative.

Time

Time moves with lightning speed on the campaign side. There is a finite period to work with a campaign clock ticking against you. In the end, either you win or lose. In a government agency setting, time moves slower. In government, policy evolves over time as opposed to a campaign which can spiral downward in a split second based on a tweet. Government employees can adjust initiatives over time by learning from the outcomes. A campaign operative has no time to understand long term effects. The only desired effect is to win at the polls. They are hired to develop short term gains yesterday. Befriend and educate them on the issues to guide them into your long-term vision. Communicate with them daily and make sure there are no surprises they will read about in the newspaper. Use your time wisely with them. Become a sounding board for them and the trust level will skyrocket.

Results

The results on the campaign side are easy to understand as you will either help your candidate win at the polls or suffer a loss. There is no room for a second shot at something which did not work right the first time. Results in the world of policy making may not come to fruition for years. When laws are passed, they evolve over time and must be tweaked to address glitches or unintended consequences. Educate the political operatives on policy making and create timelines to assess results. Have meetings on the effects of policy changes which include them. Political operatives must feel comfortable in their new roles. When asked, convey things quickly and accurately. Do not stay out of sight for more than a week. If you are not asked you will not be needed. Make sure you come up with results to deliver or you will be delivered to an unemployment line. Bring your results ahead of schedule and exceed expectations by always adding a little extra.

Team

The original team policy makers start with is usually never the same at the end of the campaign. In government, you get to know your peers over time and develop long-lasting relationships. Campaign staff comes and goes. There is no tenure, civil servant status, or pension to retire on. Give coveted appointees a reason to get to know you. You have to eliminate the "me" in the team and guide them into understanding the long-term resources available to them. Help other staff around you by introducing the political operative to their strengths and importance to your organization. Position yourself as an indispensable part of their team.

Political operatives who understand the intricacies of government agencies and benefit from your advice and mentoring will help you elevate as they move up the ladder. The ones who have no interest in learning will usually not last long and move to starting on another campaign. Nonetheless, your patience and guidance will gain respect with both.

Your Synergistic Circle

Leadership, parties, and political operatives can be a source of power, but their insecurity and political paranoia can take a lot of time to manage.

Chiragon

You have to understand their fast-paced universe before jumping to any conclusions. Appreciate your synergistic circle every second to deal with someone else's. Follow your values and develop extra patience.

Holarchy of Need

You must move to the positive in this world which assumes the negative first. Constant communication and reinforcement will bring you into a needed slot.

Brand

As you empower your agency and coworkers with the political operatives in this circle, they will acknowledge you as being part of the solution.

Chapter 9

Lifelong Staff

In the Cuban American culture, there is a saying that translates into something like this. The Devil is not smart because he is the Devil, he is smart because he has been around for such a long time.

I do not mean Lifelong Staffers are the Devil, but time made them smarter and craftier than you can ever imagine. They are also called Super Staff because of the way they survive downward spirals only to be right back on top again. Lifelong Staff is admired, hated, feared, adored, or despised depending on who you talk to. They must be respected. They are the force which helps pass legislation or will kill it. I guarantee you will come across these agile survivors. They are easy to spot. They are usually the masters of a subject area, i.e. Staff Director of a Healthcare Committee or are the longest serving Chief of Staff in a Speaker's office. You have to approach them with a great deal of care and finesse. You must impress them with knowledge of your policy area and ability to drive policy changes to get to the next level. They are the gatekeepers of the upward mobility card in agencies or departments. Below are the three main characteristics of Lifelong Staff.

Subject Matter Commander

When it comes to a policy area whether it is transportation, healthcare, insurance or the environment, there will always be a name who symbolizes the essence of knowledge in each of these areas. He or she will always be the point person for an agency head or policy maker. The Lifelong Staffers entrenched themselves in these subject matter areas by learning and understanding the historical evolution of the area better than anyone. The Lifelong Staffer has the ability to block legislative proposals they do not agree with and there will be a trail of dead bodies to prove it. It's simple, without their blessing, nothing will happen in their respective policy areas. Learn from them as their knowledge is priceless.

Mover of the Pieces

Lifelong Staffers can forecast the flow of policy and politics better than anyone. They help direct it and often orchestrate it. Lifelong Staffers are always many steps ahead of everyone else. They help position policy makers in a way that perpetuates their power. Policy makers who chair key committees will attribute their success to a Lifelong Staffer. Conversely, problem staff and policy makers who threaten their existence are disposed of with precision. A policy maker who is removed from a key committee can usually point to a Lifelong Staffer for helping to orchestrate the ouster. Become a needed piece of their universe and stay close to them in order not to lag behind their moves.

Creators of a Strong Bureaucracy

Lifelong Staff will hire younger staffers who they can mold and empower to strengthen their long-term position. They command loyalty and will either reward or penalize accordingly. They will hire and create a future tier of Lifelong Staff who they will train to

Staff has a strong force field.

be smarter and become as entrenched as they are. I see people who refuse to work with them and I am amused by the consistent outcomes. Lifelong Staff will always win.

As a staffer in the Business of Politics, you must earn the respect of Lifelong Staff and benefit from their massive amount of knowledge. They give taxpayers an incredible return on their investment. People in private enterprise who have the knowledge and capabilities of a Lifelong Staffer will earn four times as much and then some. As a staffer, you will be amazed at the wealth of knowledge you can access by working with them. Lifelong Staff keeps the process running efficiently and for the most part, protects the policy maker. They are a force to deal with and learn from.

They see dishonesty coming a mile away. Below are some tips that will help you earn the respect of Lifelong Staff and benefit from their abilities.

Patience

You must learn over time. If you try to learn too fast, you may be seen as an uncontrollable threat to the governance of Lifelong Staff. If you learn too slow, you will be phased-out before you realize what is going on. Let them coach you. They will determine the acceptable pace for you. They were once in your shoes so be patient.

Questions

Do not be afraid to ask for guidance and advice. Young staffers may be hesitant to ask for help. Lifelong Staff welcomes your questions. Your questions will help Lifelong Staff assess your strengths and weaknesses in order to help guide you in the right direction. People say there is never a stupid question, but you and I know there are questions which make you look stupid. Do not ask a question you already know the answer to. Think before you ask.

Prepare

Do your homework. There are so many resources out there. Please use them. You need to stimulate the creation of top-notch policy. Being part of the solution is paramount with Lifelong Staff. Research all angles prior to briefing them. They will be impressed by a possible outcome you identify that escaped them.

Team Approach

Take a team approach. If you come across self-centered, you will become a threat to Lifelong Staff. Use the terms "our agency," "our department," "our committee," "our leadership." Emphasize your appreciation for others. Always be thankful. Praise the team and not yourself.

Pay Attention to the Origins of Policy

Lifelong Staff will generally evolve with time to survive. The degree of evolution will vary. Strive to understand when and how to advocate changing a policy which was authored by Lifelong Staff. There will be Lifelong Staff who will have such pride any proposed changes to policy authored by them may bring resistance. Policy must evolve with your cunning. If you are charged with pursuing a policy change, work with the original Lifelong Staff who helped author what may be the model of excellence to them. Make them feel a part of the change by spending the time necessary to win them over with your reasoning. Work with Lifelong Staff on easing into change and do not propose a radical evolution until you earn a high level of respect.

The Long Life of Lifelong Staff

I angered a Lifelong Staffer back when I was 19 due to my young, cocky "me" attitude. When I started lobbying, guess who consistently worked against me? You got it, the Lifelong Staffer who I alienated. A few fellow Lifelong Staffers who did not know me, banded together to let me know I disrespected one of their brethren. It took years to repair and a ton of time I could have used to move other aspects of my life forward. The lack of sleep added up as my frustration grew. Easy client victories became client failures. I managed to work through mending and healing. I gave them praise before key politicians and anyone else who I felt would be helpful. Do not forget to use the words thank you with Lifelong Staff.

Your Synergistic Circle

Lifelong Staff provides you the ultimate source of knowledge. Earning their respect takes time and patience.

Chiragon

Make sure to approach Lifelong Staff with zero ego. A large ego will eliminate any chance you have to learn from the best. Be true to your values and continue to develop humility. Always thank them for their advice.

Holarchy of Need

The Lifelong Staff must see you as a long-term investment. When they started, someone of their caliber took time to help them evolve. Lifelong Staff should view you as a younger version of themselves when some other Lifelong Staff took the time and energy to help them grow. You will fulfill their need to give back.

Brand

Your name and stature should yield a long-term return for time spent by Lifelong Staff on you. Your branding must be so strong they will feel comfortable telling others you have a chance of even surpassing them.

Chapter 10

Press and the Media

If you are not the public information officer (PIO), city or county manager, secretary of a state or federal department or an elected policy maker, stay away from the press. The press evolved into a gotcha culture in today's fast paced information world. This culture is full of fear and our society has been trained to read the bad as the bad sells ads. There are many social media outlets and an insane number of video devices out there. The outcome of interacting with the media will most certainly place you in a gotcha scenario. Policy makers do not look to the media to write positive articles but fear the bad ones.

You will be warned to stay away from the media on day one. You will hear, "If contacted by the media, direct them to the appropriate spokesperson." If you are chosen as the spokesperson the following realities should be understood.

- Whatever you say will be with you forever.
- The info will be used both to help and hurt you personally.
- There exists no fair retraction process. Once you say it, you own it. In most cases what you said will own you.

You will probably not be asked to interact with the press until you are a seasoned staffer. This does not keep the press from trying to interact with you. Be wary of the local watering holes where policy makers, lobbyists, and politicians are known to frequent as everything from the table next to you to the stall in the restrooms should be deemed to have a listening device.

The walls have ears.

Public Information Officers (PIO) and Communications Staff

The press moves at the speed of light. Members of the press are under pressure to get "the story." Since the print media died, reporters now have to generate clicks or gain social media attention to sell advertising. The more people click on a reporter's story the more attention they will receive. They are competing with other reporters, bloggers, Facebook, Twitter, and cable news networks to be the first one to get a story which not only sells but facilitates their upward mobility. "The story" always appears on the front page while the retractions hide in the back pages like a dictator trying to hide his war crimes. Any article which names you can be detrimental. Your job is to advise the agency or policy maker on how to answer the question you so methodically deciphered. Use your resources to research the issues and set an appropriate tone for the question the agency head or policy maker is to answer. As a Public Information Officer (PIO) or a staffer in a communications capacity in the Business of Politics, you should develop the following proactive protocols to prepare for issues which will inevitably come up.

Develop Key Messages

Work with your agency's executive team or policy maker to develop a series of key messages which create real positive impacts. These messages should revolve around the needs of your community or constituency. Do not just say things to say something to them, rather talk about things you are accomplishing.

Your messages should revolve around the mission of your agency. If you work for an elected policy maker, they should revolve around delivering on campaign promises. I know this seems crazy and even unheard of nowadays.

Fear, everything is bad.

Most people do not believe any politician will deliver on their promises. Your agency or policy maker is going to be critiqued, so deliver on what you say you can deliver on. It is a simple game of addition in our social media driven world. If you get more likes than the other guys you win.

Develop a Communications Team

An effective communications team should be in place in order to diffuse adverse issues while constantly promoting the positives of your agency or policy maker. Assemble a group of your agency's leadership. Make it a habit to directly interact with them on an on-going basis. You have to be able to call upon your agency's resources to get up to the minute updates from the appropriate staff regarding the issue. Be proactive and use social media every day. This will highlight your key messages. Keep the press busy trying to find flaws against a chatter of likes that increase your positives.

Consider the following guidelines prior to releasing a response to an inquiry from the press.

A. Timeliness. Issues do not just go away so address them immediately.
B. Gather your facts before engaging the request.
C. Get the reputation of the reporter. If you do not personally know the reporter research them in addition to the issue at hand.
D. Get the scoop/focus of the story. Keep it narrow as reporters like to expand the scope.
E. Never answer, "What-Ifs."
F. Stick to interviews as opposed to just giving statements. Statements seem to always find their way into other pieces which will be used against your agency head or policy maker.

Turnover is high in the press corps as the media universe is constantly morphing. Analyze media patterns from credible sources regarding issues that are likely to affect your agency or policy maker. I guarantee you a lot of frustration as no matter how well you prepare and interact with the reporter who writes the story, the headline writer will always write the headline. Headlines attract attention, and attention attracts advertising.

Over time, you will know who the credible reporters are. Use your contact with them wisely. They are looking to get a scoop and you are looking for a resource to achieve the policy objectives that will not scoop you up into the drama.

Press Me Not

I did not know to stay away from the press and more importantly, did not realize the power of the phrase "off the record." I was working for the Commissioner of Agriculture and had a solid group of professionals around me. I was allowed to work on everything from lobbying, regulatory, and the interaction with the growing Hispanic media. Hispanic radio ruled as the medium of the day in Miami. Back then, there was no coaching on Hispanic media. The Hispanic community did not have the economic or voting power they have today. Interaction with them was an afterthought in politics. The Commissioner wanted to change this, and I was his person. Unfortunately for some parties and elected policy makers, this interaction is still an afterthought today.

I developed a segment on Consumer protection as the department regulated fuel pumps in gas stations to ensure consumers were protected. The Commissioner wanted to update the program legislatively. It needed some tweaking. The legislative director was told to secure sponsors for this effort and drafted a bill.

I, the eager beaver, got right on Hispanic radio and discussed our innovation initiative to get ahead of the curve. I was later at a local watering hole and was approached by a member of the press corps who found out about the initiative from a friend in Miami who heard me speak on the radio. He asked a myriad of questions, and I was again too eager to answer them. I never said the words "off the record." This was not a thing you said on Hispanic radio.

The following day I was asked to come to the chief of staff's office along with the legislative and communications directors. It concerned a story that might have the following headline: "Florida Commissioner of Agriculture has serious concerns about fraud committed by owners of gas stations in Hispanic Communities." The Cuban community in Miami was a coveted block of votes which all statewide elected officials needed to get in a general election. Many of the gas stations in the Hispanic community in Miami were owned by Cuban Americans.

As you could imagine, this did not bode well for my upward mobility. I tried to make sense of it and explain my way through it. The reporter who I spoke to was in the Commissioner's lobby and was waiting to discuss the story with the Chief of Staff. I was lucky back then, reporters tried to get their facts right before releasing a story. The reporter came in and met with our team. We showed him the draft legislation, as well as the issue brief detailing the reasoning behind the changes. These are called talking points today. The changes were statewide and focused on updates which recognized the new technology at the time. The reporter decided to update the story. His editor never published it. There was no scandalous value to writing about technology and plain old gas pumps.

Your Synergistic Circle

The press and the media are not friends. In the Business of Politics, they build you up to have a target to tear down. The interaction with them must be infrequent, short, and sweet.

Chiragon

Having a large ego will not help your spirit. Making the front page of some political article or social media blog that the same people in the political process read over and over again will do nothing for you as a staffer except get you unstaffed.

Holarchy of Need

Unless you are the public information officer or the communications director, there can exist no Holarchy of Need with the media.

Brand

Your name appearing in print on some political drama blog is not going to help you move up in the process. Target credible business and policy periodicals to build up your policy maker's brand at the direction of your agency or policy maker.

Chapter 11

Takers

Takers are those who take from you to a point where you have nothing left to give. Takers will always come to you with the "me, me, me, now, now, now" approach to life. They are the single largest threat to your synergistic circle. They drain your soul. The problem is we all know them yet are somehow blind to the true nature of their existence until it is too late. As a staffer in the Business of Politics, you will be exposed to Takers who usually come in two varieties.

Old Friends

Everyone should help their friends. You will see a variety of old and new friends gravitate towards you depending on your upward mobility in your respective agency or political office. You should help people across the board. You are a public servant. The problem arises when you have a recurring group of old friends who make more aggressive requests for favors over time. You have to balance the friendship with the needs of your agency or policy maker. You must tell them no, from time to time. Professionals in the process and your true friends understand and move on to the next issue.

The problem arises with the old friend who has close access to you and only thinks about himself. Just like a spoiled child who

Takers

gets everything they want all of the time. They may become a liability when told no on an issue. They may make a big dramatic deal out of it. They will vilify you with the same flair as they marketed being the closest to you. Gauge their access to you carefully. Make sure those around you provide a symbiotic relationship which enables you to grow from their tidbits of information as well as they from yours. Ask them for information and favors frequently. Things such as "I have a friend who is looking to evolve in your field and would benefit from your advice," or "Please get me the trends on a certain issue in other states. I know you are knowledgeable in this area." Go a long way to provide balance. Hold them accountable. If it is only a one-way street, you are sure to end up disappointed at some point.

New Hires

Everyone should mentor and help others. You will mentor a variety of new hires as well as old hires to get them to the next level. You want to become known as a go to mentor in your agency. Being part of the overall solution is never a bad thing. The problem arises when dealing with a Taker. There will be a series of things which should sound the alarm with this Taker category. Here are the top three.

The "I Want Your Job" Taker

This Taker will circle back with your superiors on the advice you give them from time to time. They will question your advice when they go over your head to plant doubt about you.

If this happens, you need to confront them immediately and correct this behavior. If it happens more than once, you need to assign their mentoring curriculum to HR and get rid of them.

They will belittle your wisdom and come across as having better solutions. I see this all of the time and do not get why some people do this, but they do. The right thing to do is come and ask you. They should be appreciative and loyal but Takers take.

The "I Know It All" Taker

We have all tried to help someone, typically a young Up and Coming person who has so much potential. Being young has its pros and cons when it comes to the Business of Politics. The lack of patience as we live in a now, now, now, society can be overcome as long as it is not all about me, me, me.

The new hire who wants to learn and be productive will acknowledge your advice and try to learn from it. They may be hardheaded at first, but you will see a positive progression over time. The new hire who is a Taker will immediately get angry and stay angry when you correct them. It is much like telling the spoiled kid that they cannot buy a BMW. Takers will go one step further. They will start a dialogue with others in your agency about how much smarter they are than you. You can and should confront them. I have not had success helping this kind of taker. They usually are what they are and need to be purged from your organization before they become a cancer.

The "I Know the Right People" Taker

This type of new hire has a 50/50 survival rate since, for the most part, they can be trained and taken to the next level if they listen. This new hire type will come from a winning political campaign organization, be related to a mayor, senator, or something like that. They will usually be young and have no idea what they signed up for.

You will be tasked to get them up to speed. Keep it very professional and do not socialize outside of work with them. You need to get them out of the political cocktail parties and into the process of making policy. Communicate with them as an equal at first. Make them feel good about knowing who they know but begin to switch the focus to enable them to build their substance and credibility and not just depend on someone else's. They will either work hard and listen or not. The ones who listen will rave about you to their political contacts and those who feel entitled will not. They will see you as a threat. As long as you keep it professional, you will survive the bashing. Ultimately, the entitled ones who refuse to learn will get other staff positions and eventually run out of politicians willing to help them.

Taken by Takers

I could write a whole book on Takers. My dad seemed to attract them all. I did too, early in my career. My father never hesitated to help anyone. There were many exile families who my dad mentored and helped.

I find myself challenging my Chiragon on this all of the time. I inherited my dad's ability to attract and help those in need. I welcome this challenge and blessing but am wary of those who take and do not give, unlike my dad. Some of the families who my father helped were not there during the waning days of his life two weeks before my graduation from law school. The families who were nowhere were flushed out as Takers.

I was an only child and became the primary support for my parents as I worked during my second and third years of law school. I was 500 miles away in Tallahassee and was trying to help my mother deal with my dad's worsening state of health. Thank God I had a great family and non-taker friends to help mom and dad.

In the Business of Politics, I learned to help and be a part of the solution all of the time. The Senator I worked for was surrounded by a myriad of Takers who he eventually empowered me to flush out. I made a list of people who he would continuously help and asked them to do things for the Senator. There were a few whose primary mission in life was only to give such as mental health counselors and nursing home professionals. According to the Senator, "they were on a mission from God." These were exempt as they called on the Senator to help others and not themselves.

I had a growing following of operatives who needed to get close to the Senator. I learned some of my closest friends would not reciprocate if I called on them to help the Senator with messaging, town hall meetings, and to help some of his initiatives. I asked a person who was always in the office to get a very qualified friend of the Senator a simple interview with an entity they represented. The request was never acknowledged. They simply ignored it by making excuses and delaying the matter. I gave them ample opportunity to follow up and deliver on the request. Eventually, their daily residence in the Senator's office was canceled and their subsequent requests also fell on deaf ears.

Your Synergistic Circle

Takers are the ultimate disruptors of your synergistic circle. They will hurt you personally and take a lot of time from your focus. They will poison others in the process against you. Takers can keep you awake at night worrying about their actions and how to combat them. The saving grace is Takers are easy to identify and are predictable.

Chiragon

As long as you spend time keeping yourself centered, you will be sensitive to the games Takers play. Takers will blind you with their "oh woe is me" attitude and position you into an endless cycle of being taken. Takers will be a recurring vision at bedtime if you do not move on and eliminate them from your daily life. Your Chiragon will help you snap out of their spell.

Holarchy of Need

There is no Holarchy of Need because need is one way with Takers. Takers need you to get things done. You will never need them because they will not do anything for you. The Holarchy of Need has to work both ways.

Brand

Your brand will become stronger after a few encounters with Takers. You will project a "you will not take advantage of me," aura which will be feared and admired. Takers will avoid a strong brand that can flush them out.

Chapter 12

The Little Things that Matter Big

People on their death bed never have regrets over monetary things. You see it over and over again in movies: "I wish I would have married her," or "I should have spent more time with my kids," or "I missed making so many wonderful memories because of working all of the time."

Your family and your true friends were there before you became staff and should be there as you grow in your career. My father's health rapidly declined as I moved up in Florida staff circles and I made sure I spent as much time with him as possible. Every Saturday was movie night with dad. It didn't matter who called or what was going on. I will always treasure those moments.

You see so many people in life who are great at their professions but have no personal life. Old friends slip away as you surround yourself with new ones. You do not want to be friendless. Let's not even get into relationships, as being lonely and depressed is a common theme these days. Are you lonely because you are depressed or depressed because you are lonely? How can you attract someone when all you do is work? If your spouse, best friend, work out partner, fishing buddy, movie date, dinner companion is your smartphone, you are probably going to be beyond depressed and develop some serious issues.

Your friends and family crave your company as you do theirs. I am not talking about the estranged ones in your circles. Spend time with the good ones. In the Business of Politics, things move so fast many people think there is no off switch.

I spend a lot of time consulting people in politics on simply just turning things off. Consistently turning things off will make you a better staffer and more importantly a better soul who can serve as a model for other family members, mentees and even world leaders to follow. I believe, I know, we can do better as a society and as policy makers by simply paying attention to what matters in the long run. Below are the main areas that pose serious obstacles you need to conquer in your personal life to truly become a master in the Business of Politics and beyond. Once you commit to these, you cannot cheat. You should make these habits. If you turn things back on, you will lose the benefit of the action.

Technology

Turn it off. We were promised technology would give us more time by making us more efficient. We all know, like socialism, this only works in theory. As a dad, I constantly have to tap other parents at my children's games when their child scores or makes a key play. They are on their phones, laptops or tablets getting work done or worse, they are catching up on social media when they should catch up on being a parent. When a son or daughter scores on a field or court, they always glance towards their parents. They need you to know they did it. It is so rewarding to smile, nod, or thumbs-up back. How can you miss that? Our phones have taken over our lives.

Back in the day, my wife and I would catch each other texting on our date night. Now, only one of us takes their phone in case the kids need us. For most, losing their phone is right up there with one of the worst things that can happen in life. Try turning it off on weekends. I understand there will be some weekends which require access to you due to a major project or key deadline, but every weekend cannot be that way. If you are constantly on the phone checking email, tweets and texts on the weekend, you should get dressed and go into work. Forget weekends exist. Ignore those who love you.

Stop lying to yourself and focus on your friends and family. I promise you will be a new invigorated person ready to take over the world on Monday. Try it this weekend. It will change your life.

Health

No matter how good you are at what you do, a breakdown in your physical or mental health will impede your upward mobility. Eating right, working out, and not going overboard on happy hours will serve you well. Being diagnosed with something is "life-changing," and survivors always make serious adjustments to their lifestyle if they live, don't they? You see the story on TV or read about it in social media every day. Why wait for a diagnosis? Find something that challenges you physically while also being fun. There are so many options out there. Getting a routine down with a buddy who can push you and hold you accountable is easier said than done. There is no secret fad or pill. Get moving, eat right, and work out. I just saved you a ton of money on shakes, bars and faddy work-out equipment which ends up in a garage sale.

Vacations

Today's culture frowns on vacations. Do not get me wrong. I am so grateful for my clients and coworkers. I am even more grateful they place their trust in me to service their complex needs and value not only my opinion, but my friendship. Vacations aren't directly despised, but for some reason, no one respects your space when you are on vacation. Things will always come up to disrupt your time away. Does the following sound familiar?

"Something always hits the fan right before I go on vacation."

"It's a nightmare when I get back from vacation."

You get several of these on your voicemail. "I am sorry to call you on your vacation but…"

I wrote this chapter when I was away snowboarding with my family in the Midwest and recorded my vacation greeting. "I am on vacation, and I will call you upon my return," message when I received three messages from a reporter who needed a quote on an

The little things that matter.

issue I was working on for a client. The reporter listened to my message every time they left a message but could care less about the fact I was on vacation. They left more aggressive deadline messages every subsequent time. I called them back upon my return date as designated by my voice greeting well before their deadline. I brought up the fact they left me several messages while I was enjoying my family time. I asked if he listened to my message and why he thought I would interrupt my vacation time to call him back. His reply was, "Everyone else does."

The "I am sorry to call you on your vacation, but," message means "I am sorry to call you on your vacation, but I do not care about your time off." You have to stand your ground. You must learn to depend on your organization and more importantly let go from time to time to recharge your batteries. If you agree to take a call on vacation, you are done. Everyone will ask for your time. You will be known for not walking your talk. Time off with loved ones will make you more productive in the long run. I promise.

Your Synergistic Circle

Learn to turn things off. Make time for family and friends by focusing on the moment and not being pulled away by emails, social media or phone calls.

Chiragon

Spend quality time with loved ones and take care of yourself. This is the ultimate food for your soul.

Holarchy of Need

Your loved ones need you. In life, you will need them ten-fold.

Brand

You should be looked up to as a great person who loves his family and friends. You want to be remembered as a great dad, mom, brother, sister, partner and friend. Time goes by so fast. Please do not let others consume it.

Chapter 13

Challenged Bosses

Getting ahead in life takes hard work, and there is a rite of passage for advancement. Anyone who feels they are entitled does not belong in the Business of Politics or any other business. Everyone has or will work for the Boss who has no life, no family, and only cares about getting the job done at all cost. A Challenged Boss has many internal trials which make them miserable. They strive to make others around them join their misery. The personalities always profile the same.

- They take no real vacations as they check in more when away than when in the office.
- They have no long-term friends as friends come and go.
- They typically never see their relatives.
- They always strive to come across as the victim.
- Their relationships belong in a real-life drama series.

Everyone knows who they are in your organization. They are the source of a lot of chatter as people will marvel at what they say or do to other co-workers. Their reputation will precede them.

If you get stuck with one, you will learn a ton from them because you will always be working. When they are in the office, they will expect you to be right there with them. A

Challenged Bosses

Challenged Boss will always conduct some mandatory emergency call when they know you will be on vacation. A timely project will be rammed down your throat on the eve of your daughter's wedding. They will always dangle something like a promotion to keep you going down the irrational path they design. You will never get it. The promotion will diminish the power they have over you.

A Challenged Boss thinks he is always the smartest person in the room. They try to come across as helping by having you do tasks they ask you to do. Their ego is limitless and they are the most important person in the organization as everyone else is beneath them and "Just plain stupid." There is no pleasing them, and sooner or later, you will look in the mirror and say, "I have had it."

Before you do something, you will regret, there is a strategy for dealing with these miserable souls. Listen to them and count to five before reacting to their nonsense. Let them know how important they are to you, the organization, or policy maker. Strive to impress them while catching the eye of someone else who will hire you. When planning your move never speak ill of them to others and take the high road always. Sell your capabilities and not their shortcomings. You never want to hate your profession. Working for a Challenged Boss will push you to the breaking point and not be good for your soul. There is a difference in working for a Demanding versus a Challenged Boss.

A Demanding Boss will push you to learn and help you move up in the organization. They will demand loyalty and a good work ethic which will make you a better staffer. A Challenged Boss will push you to be as cracked and as miserable as they are.

Loco Boss

I maneuvered through several Challenged Bosses. In one instance, I had a boss belittle me before other people. Cry and tell me they were going to make me a better staffer or fire me by the end of the week, while suggesting I get a raise. All this happened in under two minutes. One of my roommates worked for a Senator who would check around every time they walked into the office to make sure the office was not bugged. Another roommate worked for a State Representative who accused him of working for a political opponent because they happened to be on the same vacation aboard a cruise ship. I had a boss who wanted to drive me crazy and get me fired then invite me to his wedding. I was even asked to be in their wedding party. I can go on. If they are loco, crazy, insane, or disturbed, find another boss.

Your Synergistic Circle

A Challenged Boss is trying to make you irrational also.

Chiragon

Spend extra time focusing your center and appreciating the wonderful things in your life. Tell yourself this short-term period will end as you are becoming stronger every day. You will move on to better positions armed with a higher tolerance threshold. Looking back on this period will help you appreciate future positions.

Holarchy of Need

Challenged Bosses only need themselves and their misery. There is no need to have them need you or you to need them.

Brand

Your brand with them will fluctuate like everybody else's. You will go from amazing to worthless in a split second depending on what side of the bed they got up on. Do the best you can to be part of the solution. Keep in mind they see themselves as the only ones who can deliver the right solution all of the time. Their brand is second to none.

Chapter 14

Death of Your Chiragon
Don't Live Life Just Checking-Off Boxes

Your Chiragon is fueled by life's experiences. Your Chiragon is the interaction with everything around you, including and most importantly, your time with yourself. We tend to limit ourselves and, in the process, forget who we are.

How do you kill your Chiragon? You wake up every day with no passion, zero energy and fear. You develop an inability to pursue your dreams, not caring about all you can be. Evolving into a dreadful state of mind typically does not happen overnight. This state of existence usually takes a series of events to reach. Some get to this state in a split second when those who they care about die in a car accident or when one of their best friends gets murdered overnight.

Why go through life with no passion? No one is immune from getting to this state. I got there after my dad died. I just went through daily motions and checked off a box. I touched base with my girlfriend at the time to avoid any drama by not calling. I dragged myself to meetings and took many things for granted. I was unable to see anything as wonderful or inspiring. I know many people who live life just checking off a box. Does the following sound familiar?

- I need to check in with my wife before she divorces me.
- I have to call my boss, or I may get fired.
- Let me check in with my mom before she calls me to let me know I have not called her.
- If I do not check in with my business partner the office will call the police.
- Let me call my children to let them know I am still alive.

These are just some examples of living a lie. How can any of the above scenarios create spiritual growth? We hear these scenarios way too often from others who we care about. The real problem exists when we hear this from ourselves. You can always help others when you have your Chiragon in check.

Your Chiragon is everything. In the first chapter of this journey, I defined your Chiragon as "A life force that moves your spirit." In life, we will all have periods of ups and downs that peak to create the next phase in life. What if you have no ups, downs, or peaks? Some people call it a plateau.

I call it the death of your Chiragon. How do you come back to life? There is no magic, no pill, or quick solution. You have to get up and try something new until you get your Chiragon back. As long as you do not give up, the light will start to shine at the end of this dark chapter. You will always look back and be grateful for what you have today.

The Business of Politics is not for everyone. It is an intoxicating roller coaster full of highs and lows for a young staffer. For older, more seasoned staff, it's still a roller coaster ride. They have the tools to adapt. If you find yourself in a rut, ask yourself if you are living life or just checking off boxes.

Checking Off Eradication

Checking off a person means to treat them like a thing. You have lost your passion or feelings for them. They are just there and a part of a routine you follow because you have decided to settle for less. Have you become a person dead to your surroundings? Are you self-centered, ice cold and have no desire to deal with people? If you find yourself in this predicament, make a list of the people you treat this way and how often you do it. Chart it, excel it, or write it on a napkin. Keep it handy and catch yourself as you try to check them off again.

The next step is to ask why you are checking this person off? What can you do to make it better? Come up with different ways to communicate with them. Ask others who have a successful approach to this individual for advice. It will serve as a form of therapy to help guide you through this period. You have done this many times before in a simpler setting, but you are so caught up in the Business of Politics that you can't remember. Have you ever asked your boyfriend's best friend for advice on dealing with him? How about your girlfriend's sister to give you pointers before asking her out? Have fun figuring the person you are checking off out. You will find out a lot more about yourself.

As a young staffer, I spent a lot of time trying to figure out how to get to know others and expand my network. Increasing my circles of influence created more avenues for promotions and knowledge. If you find yourself in a dead state where you feel you do not need to get to know anyone else and do not like those around you, maybe you have lost your Chiragon.

A Dark Place

A few years after my father died, I found myself having trouble getting up in the morning. I felt alone and nothing excited me. I knew I was depressed but continued to keep things to myself. I just wanted to crawl into a cave and be left alone. I went through the routine of life with no emotion or passion. Everyday became "I will get to this tomorrow day."

My physical self changed also. I gained some weight and felt tired all of the time. Going to the office did not excite me like before. I immediately went into my office and closed the door. My to do list was never done, and my work product suffered. Friends and family noticed it and offered their help, but I rejected it. Going to the movies to engulf myself in the empty drama of others gave me comfort but offered no solutions. I looked in the mirror and did not like what I saw and just rolled with it until I had a conversation with an old high school friend. I bumped into him at the mall when I was home for the holidays. They told me how proud they were of me. They read about me in an article. They were caught up in a dull routine after dropping out of college and praised me for getting to law school and making it big. Something snapped in me. I smiled and gave them a hug.

The next morning, I got to work. I created a spreadsheet listing my family members, friends, co-workers and people I needed to get to know. Next to their names I listed the following:

- How to get or better get, to know them?
- Last Interaction
- Next Interaction
- How do I feel about them?

I populated the list and felt my passion come back slowly but surely. I began to get excited about waking up again. The morning and night routines which had evaded me for a few months in the Business of Politics were found again. My network grew and I was given additional responsibilities. One of the additional duties required me to work with several consultants who still send me client referrals today. Lastly, I started dating an incredible person. My Chiragon was restored.

Your Synergistic Circle

Your Chiragon is dying if you are in a state where you have stopped caring and evolving.

Chiragon

Feed your soul by successfully communicating with those who you are checking off.

Holarchy of Need

If you just check others off in life, your need is empty, and emptiness is what you will get in return.

Brand

While you cannot please everyone all of the time you certainly cannot alienate everyone all of the time. Others have to gravitate towards you. You must provide that avenue. Plant the seeds to enable relationships to grow.

Chapter 15

Conclusion

I started this book series back when I was in law school over 20 years ago. I used to beat myself up for not writing it earlier. Now that the first book is completed, I understand why it took such a long time. The knowledge I shared required more of life's experiences. I needed more time to arm you with the tools to help you succeed.

Today, I am a partner in one of the fastest growing Government Relations firms in the country. My partners and our staff share a deep commitment to client service and value the wisdom and guidance provided by staff. As we formulate business and policy solutions for our clients, we do not forget where we came from as most of the members of the firm started as staff. I coach policymakers and their staff on a daily basis. I enjoy helping others to get to the next level.

It is your turn. The policy making mechanics in this book must be mastered by you. Start with your inner self. Take some time for you as a daily habit. Document your failures as well as your successes. Envision you reaching your goals and realizing your dreams. Our goals are achieved by taking action. The Business of Politics has many pitfalls and obstacles not found in everyday life.

There is so much fear in our world. As I finish this final chapter, I am home with my family during the 2020 COVID-19 pandemic. The media hype alone is driving everyone crazy. I have chosen to focus on the positives in our society and influence what I can control. Client service has soared to a new high. My firm adapted to provide a new level of service for our clients most affected by the current pandemic. We refused to let the times rob us from an ability to provide added value to our clients, families and each other. My physical training has increased along with the mental nourishment of my Chiragon. No matter what surrounds you, *The Business Of Politics Series* should help you conquer your fears and marvel at what you have accomplished when you look back.

I hope to get to know you one day as you evolve in the Business of Politics. Please share your experiences with those around you in the policy making process. Teaching others is the best way to master these techniques. It will take your Chiragon to a higher place as you help others help themselves. Maybe I will be reading your book some day that will help my upward mobility.

Quick Reference Guide

Branding: An ever-evolving promotion of the services you can provide by building a brand based on credibility, a smart work ethic and creating an aura about you which causes others to gravitate towards you as a crucial part of the solution. (See also: Operational Branding Protocol, Sensational Branding Protocol, and Toxic Brands)

Check Box Eradication:

How to get or better get to know them
Last Interaction
Next Interaction
How do I feel about them?

Chiragon: Why you do the things you do which guide your spirit (See also: Synergistic Silos)

Considerations for Responding to the Press:

Timeliness. Issues do not just go away so address them immediately.

Gather your facts before the engaging request. Do nothing on the fly.

Get the reputation of the reporter. If you do not personally know the reporter research them in addition to the issue at hand.

Get the scoop/focus of the story and stick to it. Reporters like to expand the scope.

Never answer, "What-Ifs."

Stick to interviews as opposed to just giving statements. Statements always find their way into other pieces which will be used against your agency head or policy maker.

EVENING: Your evening routine. **E**valuate, **V**ictories, **E**nvision, **N**ews, **I**ntelligence, **N**eutralize, **G**ame plan (See also: MORNING)

Holarchy of Need: In a Holarchy of Need, every person has value as a part of a whole which cannot exist without each individual part. The parts are crucial and create the whole, which is the sum of the parts.

Inner Circle: Family, Locals, Contributors, Parties, Scouts, Friends, Politicians

RACCPIN: The daily habits to reinforce your value with a policy maker. **R**einforce, **A**sk, **C**onnect, **C**orrect, **P**raise, **I**nteraction, **N**o

MONEY: The five types of financial players in the Business of Politics. **M**ajor Donors, **O**ld Money, **N**ew Money, **E**ntrenched Positioners, and the **Y**oung Up-and-Coming

MORNING: Your morning routine. **M**e, **O**rder of business, **R**elate, **N**ews, **I**ntelligence, **N**ominations, **G**uide (See also: EVENING)

Operational Branding Protocol (OBP): Under the radar, no pics, no social media, commercial-free, get-the-job-done style of Branding. The glory solely belongs to the policy maker. Under this protocol, Your Brand will earn a level of credibility which will be respected by your policy maker. (See also: Branding, Sensational Branding Protocol, and Toxic Brands)

Sensational Branding Protocol (SBP): The post it, Snap it, Instagram it, Tweet it, write a book about it, super bowl commercial style of Branding. Under this protocol, your brand projects a level of credibility which will be respected by your targeted audience who surround the policy maker. (See also: Branding, Operational Branding Protocol, and Toxic Brands)

Synergy: the constant interaction of fine-tuned elements when balanced and properly integrated create a global effect which enables you to succeed no matter how many elements come your way (See also: Synergistic Silos)

Synergistic Silos: Your Chiragon, Your Holarchy of Need, and Your Brand

Toxic Brands

1. I am, the smartest person in the room brand.
2. I am, the brand name that calls you all sorts of names.
3. I am, the have fun not helping you brand.
4. I am, the more powerful than the policy maker I work for brand.
5. I am, the only loyal to myself brand.
6. I am, the gossip and drama brand.
7. I am, world owes me something brand.

About the Author

Carlos M. Cruz has extensive policy communications and public relations experience. He served as a legislative assistant for the pro-tempore of the Florida Senate. His years of service enabled him to become well versed on a variety of local, state and national policy issues. Following his tenure in the Florida Senate, Carlos served as executive assistant to a member of Florida's elected Cabinet. As the youngest member of the Commissioner of Agriculture's executive staff, he enabled the department to communicate Florida's agricultural importance in the newly developing areas of Latin America and other Caribbean nations. Carlos has close relationships with legislators and staff as a former staffer in both the legislative and executive branches of Florida government.

He worked for various firms creating and managing their state government and policy communications practice teams. He earned a reputation of being an informed advocate who creates consistent solutions for his strong client base. Carlos's ability to work with public opinion leaders and policy maker's created a relational synergy that produces favorable outcomes. "I had to work my way up from waving on street corners for candidates as my family had no political ties. My father was a carpenter who exiled from Cuba and started from scratch in the U.S. in his mid-40's."

Candidates and policy makers rely on Carlos's experience for advice on politics, public relations campaigns, and policy trends. He is an accomplished speaker and is frequently invited to educate executives and future policy makers on the process of government relations and policy communications. "I love to give back to others and contribute positively to their development as so many have contributed to mine. Showing others how to communicate to create positive outcomes is my passion."

In addition to his government affairs practice, Carlos evolved as a crisis management consultant and is a certified life coach. He assists clients and their public relations teams with message development and corporate communications with an emphasis in Hispanic markets. As a life coach, Carlos has coached extensively and has been instrumental in helping clients in the political process find themselves again. Carlos's Synergistic Circle alignment process revolutionized the world of politics and beyond. *The Business of Politics Series* pioneers the political self-help genre.

He lives with his family in Fleming Island and enjoys turning things off to spend time with his wife and two boys. "You need to have a balance in life. Unfortunately, a lot of people in the world of politics do not seem to get that."

About the Author

Carlos has a Bachelor's degree from Florida International University in Public Administration and a Juris Doctorate from the Florida State University College of Law.

Email: carlos@cruzco.com
Follow Carlos on Twitter: @cmcruz
Instagram: @carloscruzconcepts
Facebook: @carloscruzconcepts
LinkedIn: linkedin.com/company/carloscruzconcepts
Snapchat: ccruzfl